The Palladians

Published in association with
The Royal Institute of British Architects
Drawings Collection

John Harris

The Palladians

Trefoil Books, London

My daughter Georgina wanted a book dedicated to her
and that is my pleasure here

Published by
Trefoil Books Ltd.,
7 Royal Parade,
Dawes Road,
London sw6

The publishers wish to acknowledge the generous
support of the Headley Trust in the preparation
and production of this book.

ISBN 0 86294 000 1 (paperback)
ISBN 0 86294 001 X (hardback)

Set in Monophoto Baskerville
and printed by BAS Printers Limited,
Over Wallop, Hampshire

Contents

Contents

Contents

Foreword

The Royal Institute of British Architects is very proud to be the custodian of its incomparable British Architectural Library, of which the Drawings Collection forms an important part. In scope the Collection is the largest and most comprehensive body of architectural designs in the world, with a quarter of a million drawings from the Renaissance to the present day. It is naturally orientated towards British drawings, great numbers of them presented by the architects themselves, but it contains also some magnificent continental groups, notably the Drummond Stewart collection of baroque theatre designs and the Burlington Devonshire collection which includes almost all the surviving drawings of Palladio, perhaps the most influential architect in history.

The Collection is exhaustively organised, but the use made of it by the whole international community imposes very considerable pressures on the RIBA, for published catalogues are of necessity costly. I was delighted, therefore, when the Headley Trust asked us to find a way to produce a number of illustrated books to make the treasures of the Collection known to a wider public, and to follow this by travelling exhibitions on some of the themes selected.

The fruit of this enlightened patronage is the present series of substantially illustrated books, each supported by a scholarly text, on widely different aspects of the Collection. I am confident that they will give as much pleasure to others as they have given to me.

Owen Luder
President, Royal Institute of British Architects

Preface

These thematic picture books are meant to introduce a wider public to the riches of the Collection. They are intended to explore themes with drawings, but as far as possible a conscious attempt has been made to display the beauties of architectural draughtsmanship. I have selected a wide spectrum of the most important and characteristic Palladian and neo-Palladian designs from those of the famous Inigo Jones to the obscure Esau Reynolds of Trowbridge, that is, from about 1615 to about 1750. The latter is a convenient terminating point at the mid century when architecture was still neo-Palladian rather than neo-Classic. On a matter of terminology, Palladian refers to the architecture of Jones and Webb, derivative from that of Palladio; but neo-Palladian refers to the architecture of Colen Campbell *et al*, because this was a distinct revival. Naturally, no picture book of this size could attempt to survey Palladio's influence throughout Britain, and in any case this Collection, despite its scope, possesses no drawings by Isaac Ware or Giacomo Leoni, or by Lord Pembroke and Roger Morris. I have therefore cheated a little by introducing drawings from other collections in the introduction, and by a few topographical or measured drawings in the main body of illustrations. This book has enabled me to gather my material together as a trial run for the Andrew W. Mellon lectures at the National Gallery of Art in Washington in 1981, and these lectures will form the core of my book on Palladianism and neo-Palladianism in Britain that will follow the lectures. I have relied a great deal on Howard Colvin's *Biographical Dictionary of British Architects* in its new edition of 1978, for the wisdom and erudition in his entries are profound.

John Harris

ANDREAS PALLADIVS VICENTINVS.

Portrait of Palladio, engraved by Picart in 1716
after a lost original by Veronese, from Leoni's
edition of the *Quattro Libri*

Introduction

Inigo Jones (1573–1652; see p. 13) and John Webb (1611–1672) were, therefore, Palladians, in that they introduced the Palladian style into England; Andrea Palladio died in 1586 and his pupil and assistant Vicenzo Scamozzi in 1617, whereas Colen Campbell (1676–1729) and Richard Boyle, 3rd Earl of Burlington (1694–1753; see p. 19) were neo-Palladians, who were concerned to revive the architecture and art of Palladio, Scamozzi, Jones and Webb after a hiatus of fifty years. As shall be seen, by the 18th century Scamozzi and Webb were forgotten architects who might never have existed, despite the fact that their work was as seminal to neo-Palladianism as that of their revered masters. For England, Palladio's influence before 1615 was almost entirely through the medium of his great treatise, *I Quattro Libri dell' Architettura* of 1570, and in the plans and decoration of late Elizabethan and early Jacobean buildings this influence is rarely discernible, and then usually through secondary sources. Just occasionally an Elizabethan surveyor such as John Thorpe drew out a theoretical plan that reflected an idle curiosity in Palladio's woodcuts, or perhaps an advanced element in planning such as the hall entered directly on axis as at Charlton House, Greenwich (*c.* 1607) might have been a response to Palladio's logical room systems. It is more likely, however, that these room arrangements, so novel to English architecture, were inspired by Sebastiano Serlio's six-part pattern book, *L'Architettura* 1537–1551, with its *Libro Estraordinario* of 1575, much used as a quarry by the Elizabethans. The difference between a borrowing from Serlio by Thorpe and one by Jones, who happily plundered his Serlio, is that Jones always refined and improved upon the model.

The architectural books more familiarly found in the libraries of courtiers are, in addition to Serlio, Philibert De l'Orme's *Nouvelles Inventions* of 1561 and *Architecture* of 1567, Jacques Androuet du Cerceau's *Livre d'Architecture* of 1559 and *Des plus excellents bastiments de France* of 1576–1579, and, of course, Vitruvius's *De architectura* of 1486, first illustrated in 1511, although this last-named was often in libraries by virtue of its recognition as a classical text.

As Shakespeare was born in 1564 he was a contemporary of Jones, and in view of Jones's great reputation as a designer of masques from 1605, the two must surely have met. Like Shakespeare, the early life of our 'British Vitruvius' as Webb called him (although Jones would have preferred 'British Palladio'), is shrouded in mystery. For the son of a poor man, powerful patronage must have been required, especially as Webb stated that Jones spent 'many years' studying the 'Arts of Design' on a first visit to Italy. It is possible that Jones was an Elizabethan homosexual and his time in Italy from about 1598 to 1602 or 1603 had something to do with the dandified and intellectual circle of the Earl of Essex in Venice and the Earl of Southampton, as well as the 5th Earl of Rutland, and perhaps more particularly that Earl's brother, Francis Manners, Lord Roos, who was to become the 6th Earl. It is the 5th Earl's accounts that provide that first mention of 'Henygo Jones, a picture maker' in 1603, the payment being connected with Rutland and Jones in Copenhagen where they were recorded feasting with King Christian IV at a ceremony à propos Rutland's presentation of the Order of the Garter to the king, whose sister, it should be remembered, was James Ist's queen, known as Queen Anne of Denmark.

From 1604 the Queen is Jones's great patroness, but for the theatre, not as yet for architecture. Jones may never have studied architecture during those first years in Italy, although there is that tantalising inscription made by an admirer in 1606 that through Jones's endeavours 'sculpture, modelling, architecture, painting, acting and all that is praiseworthy in the elegant arts of the ancients may one day find their way across the Alps into our England'. It would be a happy event if something concretely architectural could be ascribed to Jones during that tragic brief flowering of the court of Henry, Prince of Wales between 1610 and 1612, but we only know that in the court Jones had a rival, no less than an eminent Florentine architect, called Costantino de Servi, who had the Prince lived might well have become the royal Surveyor instead of Jones. The earliest architectural designs by Jones can be dated to about 1608 and are curious unexecuted projects for a new Exchange and for the completion of the central tower of old St Paul's Cathedral, both made up of a hotch-potch of sources from Serlio and Sangallo, although the sequence of three 'Palladian' openings in St Paul's tower are taken from Palladio's Basilica in Vicenza, via the books of Palladio or Serlio. Palladio at last has been insinuated into Britain, but this is not yet Jones the Palladian, for his ambitions to excell in architecture and to re-interpret Palladio did not occur for another five years. Jones's reputation was still as a designer of masques, but already one of European importance, and it is worth pointing out that he was also probably the finest draughtsman in England, and even at this time acquiring a connoisseurship of old master prints, particularly of the Bolognese school. He loved to collect Parmigianino, the Carracci and Guercino. Webb probably conveys a contemporary opinion of Jones's skill at drawing when he writes that he 'was not to be equalled by whatever great Masters in his Time, for Boldness, Softness, Sweetness and Sureness in his Touches'.

Just as Italy in the late 1590s was to be a climacteric for Jones the painter, so the second Italian voyage from April 1613 in the company of the Earl of Arundel was a crucial event. It confirmed Jones's unique place in English art as a top-rate renaissance artist and brought him to the watershed of becoming a renaissance architect, of a type that England had never yet produced, and of a calibre that would match Palladio. This may have been the period in his life when he began to read deeply and amply annotate books: Palladio, Serlio, Vitruvius, Lorini (on fortification) Lomazzo in Vicenza (on perspective), and in Venice he bought his Palladio (as Lord Burlington would) so as to visit Palladio's buildings, comparing them with the text and woodcuts. All this dwindles into insignifance by the astonishing event in Venice around August 1615. There he met Vicenzo Scamozzi, who only had a year to live and was possibly ill and partly blind. Jones's coup was to acquire all of Palladio's designs for private and public architecture, and possibly all of Scamozzi's, although the latter were tragically to disappear from Lord Arundel's collections in the 1650s or 1660s. The reverberations of this acquisition were to echo through British, Irish and American architecture across the next two centuries. It is worth commenting at this point that Palladio's drawings passed with those by Jones to John Webb, then the collection, by now including Webb's own drawings, was split up, with half of Jones and Webb and most of Palladio passing to John Oliver, thence to William and John Talman, thence to Lord Burlington. The other half went eventually to Dr George Clarke and so to Worcester College, Oxford; and in the meantime Burlington had found Palladio's drawings of Roman antiquity in Italy and re-united them. This celebrated collection passed to the Dukes of Devonshire and when given to the Royal Institute of British Architects in 1894 became known as the Burlington–Devonshire Collection.

Jones did not return to England during the winter of 1614 a fully fledged Palladian. A time was needed for assimilation, but a turning-point was the death in September 1615 of Simon Basil, the old Surveyor General of the King's Works – old in more than age, for this was an event to mark the transition from the traditional late Elizabethan/Jacobean style of architecture to the new Italianate. Although Jones was now in control as the royal Surveyor, not all his works from 1615 to 1617 could be described as Palladian, for they were transitional in character and in hints of eclecticism their sympathies seem to lie as close to the world of Augsburg's northern classicism as to Venice. Indeed there is the possibility that Jones visited Augsburg in 1613. The style of the new Surveyor has been determined by the Queen's House at Greenwich (Figs 3,5,6) begun in 1616, but in fact the true picture has tended to become distorted because of over-publicity from *Vitruvius Britannicus* in 1715 until the present day. Work on the Queen's House was discontinued at the level of the first floor string course late in 1618 and abandoned when Queen Anne died in 1619. The building was only finished between 1630 and 1635 for Queen Henrietta Maria, and this finishing must surely represent a recasting of Jones's ideas on the high plane of his career, rather than be the unlikely, repetitive continuation of the designs laid down in 1616, when Jones was struggling to achieve an architectural idiom. This is not to minimise the profound influence exerted by the Queen's House as a prominent suburban palace from the 1640s, for in one sense it was the first of the many Palladian villas on the Thames, the location and model *par excellence* for the neo-Palladian house, and Greenwich was a port of entry for visitors. Through dissemination in *Vitruvius Britannicus* its forty-foot cubic hall surrounded by a balustraded gallery provided the likes of Colen Campbell with the model for the hall at Houghton Hall, Norfolk (Fig. 147) in 1722, and from John Webb onwards it was quarried for its parts: the south front loggia or portico *in antis*, or the arched central north front window, were incorporated into innumerable neo-Palladian buildings (for example, see Fig. 17).

The reaction of the ordinary man to what was being built at the Queen's House can be fairly judged by the description of it in June 1617 as a 'curious devise', a phrase that could equally well have referred to the ingenious bridge-plan across the public way that divided palace precinct from park as to its astonishing classicality in the context of the old-fashioned Jacobean court style of Simon Basil. Likewise Londoners in 1619 must have been filled with wonderment at the new Banqueting House (Plate XII) rising phoenix-like out of the ruins of the old one, so Italianate was it in contrast to the medieval and later muddle of the sprawling palace of Whitehall. The Banqueting House was too idiosyncratic to be used as a model, but again its influence was as a quarry for elements: windows, doors, ceiling compartition and the grammar of its decoration. Its great double cube, galleried hall was not so easily incorporated even into grand country houses, although there was one in the north wing of Wilton after the fire of 1704, if not before. Although Jones's mandate was to replace the old Banqueting House for the enactment of masques and plays, he obviously had his eye on the future when a new palace might replace the old one. Therefore he certainly conceived his room as a *sala grande* that would easily fit as a unit in a larger whole. This may explain why his elevational solutions for the Whitehall front progressed from a straight-forward pedimented portico treatment to one of superimposed orders where axiality was minimised. Not surprisingly Jones's first design for the Banqueting House is but one step away from his recent experiences at Newmarket in Suffolk where he had just built one of the seminal buildings of the whole decade, if not the whole century.

Newmarket, then as now, was a place for the racing. The old palace had already claimed the attention of Simon Basil, and in 1615 to 1616 two of Jones's earliest royal works had been a brew house (Fig. 121), a tautly-disciplined Scamozzian design, and a stable (Fig. 120), the design for which was beautifully and freely drawn as if for a masque, and appropriately rustic, more in the spirit of Giulio Romano than Palladio. In 1619 Charles, Prince of Wales, was to be provided with a new lodging, called the Prince's Lodging, not on the site of the old palace, but nearby in the town, occupying a corner site. This was not a country house, rather a town one, but Jones's two elevation solutions for

Self-portrait of Inigo Jones, probably late 1630s, the architect in his fifties. Sepia pen (170 × 132)

the main front (Plate XI, figs 1,2) form the model for the Restoration house as well as marking a point of departure for John Webb's own great contribution to country house iconography in the shape of Gunnersbury House, Middlesex (Fig. 17), conveyed through *Vitruvius Britannicus*. If any work by Jones could be disinterred from oblivion, surely it should be Newmarket, for how tantalising it would be to see the interiors. There exists, however, one compensation in Raynham Hall, Norfolk (Figs 7,8) building from about 1621 and being assembled by its owner Sir Roger Townsend and his mason William Edge, if not under some friendly supervision from Jones, then utilising Jones's drawings for Newmarket and for other projects made in the few years before 1621. Raynham is a noble thing and is really all we have in order to re-create what a country house by Jones might have looked like. It is our Villa Maser, and its great classical portico and towering gabled wings are striking in a way that exceeds even Wilton. It is a reflection on

Campbell's selectivity in *Vitruvius Britannicus* that Raynham was never engraved, but then perhaps it was too remote, although it could have appeared in the third volume, 1725, when Campbell was at work nearby at Houghton.

Although Colen Campbell published what he regarded as the most important buildings by Jones, and under Lord Burlington's auspices William Kent performed a similar function for Jonesian drawings in 1727, it is surprising that the Queen's Chapel at St James's was never included. Burlington may have intended this because Henry Flitcroft drew a fine section of this (Fig. 136) and a plan of the Somerset House chapel ceiling (Fig. 137). It is at St James's that the 'Palladian' window appears in Jones's work for the first time.

In 1623, at one stroke, Jones produced the model for countless churches, mostly of the Wren and Georgian periods, with a box-like nave, vaulted or otherwise, a west gallery, and the Palladian window in the east end. This appears at old Stanmore church, Middlesex, by Nicholas Stone as early as 1632. During these years of the 1620s Jones's ornamental sources tend to be bookish, relying upon the engraved works of Palladio, Labacco (*Libro di Architettura*, 1552), Serlio and Vitruvius for the grammar of his constructions. The St James's Chapel demonstrates this with its barrel-vault of coffered timber based upon the Temple of Venus in Rome as published by Palladio.

A comparison with the Somerset House Chapel also shows that during the intervening ten years Jones had enlarged his vocabulary in a way that seems to indicate a release from the constraints of bookishness. Some of the interiors of the Queen's House in the 1630s (Fig. 140) and in Somerset House, as well as in the chapel there (Fig. 138) were tinctured with North Italian mannerist sources as well as displaying an interest in contemporary French interior design. The latter may have been determined by Queen Henrietta Maria herself, who seems to have required Jones to execute designs supplied by anonymous French architects, but there is also evidence at this time of a new freedom in the choice and selection of decorative and ornamental motifs, many of which can be found in earlier masques, and this is particularly demonstrated by the general character of the Somerset House chapel.

One of the great enigmas, and there are many, in an account of Jones's career, is whether he actually drew out designs for a royal palace either on the site of Whitehall or in St James's Park. All the Whitehall projects are drawn by Webb (see Fig. 24) and in terms of maturity of draughtsmanship they can hardly be dated much before 1635 and many of them are after Jones's death, and even possibly after 1660. The 'P' scheme, believed to be nearest to what Jones might have built, has little in the concordance of its elements with what Jones had designed before. It is certainly conceived as an assemblage of small units, and in this matter there is no doubt that Jones the painter did not possess the bravura needed to orchestrate a big design; but then he was not a baroque architect, and it would be left to Webb to begin to learn how

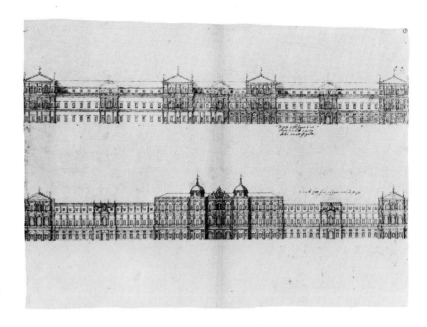

River front and park elevations for a palace of Whitehall, the 'P' scheme, attributed to Jones, drawn by Webb, but probably also designed by Webb. 1630s and later. Pen and pencil. *Courtesy Trustees of the Chatsworth Settlement*

to handle giant orders (Fig. 21) and to create depth and shadow in the modelling of his facades. Jones's abilities can best be judged by small units: a room, a moderate facade, and more than anything else by his manipulation for gateways and entrances (Figs 9–14) which are wonderfully fertile refinements and permutations upon models in his Serlio, Francini (for example the *Livre d'Architecture* of 1631), Francart (*Premier Livre d'Architecture*, 1616) or Vignola.

Jones was an undisputed genius, and geniuses are notoriously difficult to categorize. His position in the court was a privileged one, and this was astonishing in any case for a poor man's son. He was certainly an arbiter of taste and in his wide-ranging renaissance connoisseurship he was something of an *eminence grise* to many collectors, not the least the Earl of Arundel and the 3rd Earl of Pembroke. This profoundly great man totally overshadowed his contemporaries, many of whom, especially his subordinates in the Office of Works, failed to comprehend his invention. For this very reason, it is not possible to single out one building during Jones's reign as Surveyor that completely measures up to the standards and creativeness of design displayed by one of Jones's own buildings. Just as his officers of the Works were subordinates in that heirarchy, so were their own designs made for the numerous courtiers of that tragic first Stuart court. There would have been, however, one exception, and that was John Webb, and had there been no Civil War, Webb would have succeeded Jones as Surveyor in 1652; thus

Palladianism might have been prolonged well into the 1680s, and out of this might have developed a form of baroque classicism closer to Palladio's late works.

Webb has been sadly demoted in the roll call of great British architects. Brought up by Jones, to whom he was distantly related, as an amanuensis and pupil from the late 1620s, the presence of the great master was probably so overshadowing that Webb failed to acquire an identity in the 1630s. From the time of his first executed and independent commission, the reconstruction of the interiors in the south front of Wilton for the 4th Earl of Pembroke from 1648, until his last work, the new palace at Greenwich for Charles II, discontinued in 1669, he never appeared on the public stage. After his death in 1672 he was forgotten. His tragedy was that, as Britain's first professional architect, his works just before and after the Restoration in 1660 show that he was beginning to unshackle himself from Jones's grip. If he entered Jones's employ in 1627 at the age of seventeen, he could hardly have been expected to assume any executive responsibilities much before about 1635, and by 1640 the period of Jones's royal works was at an end. Webb might have assisted on the Bagshot and Hyde Park Lodges of 1631 and 1634 respectively, and possibly the last works for Queen Henrietta Maria at Wimbledon House, Surrey, from 1640. The bleakest period must have been the early 1650s, in the years after Jones's death, and this may have been the time when Webb attempted to canonize Jones through the making of many drawings for a projected treatise. There is not a shred of evidence that Jones ever contemplated such a treatise in his lifetime, and indeed such an academic exercise may well have been anathema to him. The Cromwellian Interregnum gave Webb time for reflection and perhaps even time for the first really considered study of Palladio's drawings (and perhaps Scamozzi's) in Jones's collection. It is a fascinating game to attempt to recognize among Webb's many sketch plans and elevations copies of lost designs by Palladio and Scamozzi.

Webb's achievement was to transmit Jones's court style through the gloomy years of the Protectorate, years when artisan builders came to the fore at the expense of court sophisticates. If John Penruddock's 'lodge' at Hale Park, Hampshire (Fig. 15), had been built to Webb's designs in 1638 it would have been the first documented Palladian villa in England, although there is evidence that the royal lodges at Bagshot and Hyde Park were also villas. When William Kent published the Hale designs in 1727 poor Webb's authorship had been forgotten and it was engraved under Jones's name. This was to be Webb's fate with his unexecuted designs for Belvoir Castle, Rutland (Fig. 16) and likewise in Campbell's *Vitruvius Britannicus* where he was denied his rights with Gunnersbury House, Middlesex (Fig. 17) of about 1658, Amesbury Abbey, Wiltshire (compare Fig. 18) of about 1658, the Charles II Block at Greenwich (Fig. 21), all three ascribed to Jones but 'executed by Webb', and the gallery at Somerset House (Fig. 30). Greenwich, Amesbury, Gunnersbury and Somerset House survived into the age of

neo-Palladianism, so as existing exemplars, as well as featuring in neo-Palladian literature, Webb's works are even more important than Jones's, especially in view of the fact that Newmarket, Jones's great seminal achievement, was demolished before the 1670s. Webb's importance cannot be over-estimated. Amesbury and Gunnersbury provided fundamental models for the likes of William Benson and Colen Campbell to emulate; the Charles II Block (Fig. 21) hints in its scale and in the handling of giant orders at the emergent baroque, and it is sometimes forgotten just how crucial it was in determining Wren's designs for converting and enlarging an incomplete royal palace into a Royal Hospital for Seamen. The Gallery at Somerset House became the prototype of one particular brand of elevational treatment for the neo-Palladian town house as at Leoni's Queensberry House of 1721, and it was honoured in meticulous neoclassical terms by Sir William Chambers in his Strand Block to new Somerset House of about 1776.

Webb's most precious gift must surely be the suite of apartments comprising the Single and Double Cube rooms at Wilton. There and only there can we experience the ambience of a Stuart court interior in all its gilded and painted richness: and if Webb really added the pavilion towers to Isaac de Caus's south front of about 1636 (Figs 27,28) then he initiated a type in England that was to become one of the most frequently copied Palladian models in the 18th century. Wilton was, of course, regarded as the *ne plus ultra* of all Jones's buildings, and its pavilions, its window relationships, and its elements, became fodder for the likes of Campbell and innumerable others.

If Webb was demoted by posterity, there was likewise little satisfaction for him at the Restoration. Described by John Evelyn in 1661 as 'Inigo Jones's man' he had all the qualifications to take his rightful place as the Surveyor General of the King's Works under Charles II. Disgracefully, Sir John Denham, an architectural nonentity, got the job, and when he died in 1669 Webb was again slighted by the appointment of Sir Christopher Wren. These events are merely the reflection of a new architectural situation brought about by the winds of change in architectural taste. Hugh May's Eltham Lodge of 1664 or Berkeley House, Piccadilly, of 1665, are proof of new influences from Holland and France which would soon overwhelm Anglo-Palladianism and establish the style of the Restoration and Williamite courts. Jones was now to be devalued and Palladio was out in the cold for the next half a century.

During the years of Wren's Surveyorship up to about 1700 there is not one design that can be called Palladian, except perhaps in minor episodes in a larger whole or in certain room arrangements. All Webb's achievements seemed at naught, although many of his country commissions like The Vyne in Hampshire (Fig. 19) where he achieved the first portico in British architecture could hardly have become common knowledge. He retired to his tiny Italianate seat at Butleigh Court, Somerset, acquired in 1653 (Fig. 20), and when he died there, the major part of his 'Prints and cutts and drawings of Architecture' was eventually to pass into the possession of William and John Talman. William was the arch-country house architect of the Williamite court who designed houses of astonishing variety and originality. He might have acquired the Palladio–Jones–Webb collection in 1701 and if so, it is perhaps not surprising that some of his designs for a Trianon at Hampton Court (Fig. 32) betray Palladian influences, but even so, this is minor and insignificant: Talman remained an eclectic, baroque architect.

The fount for the introduction of neo-Palladianism was not in the Talman collection, for that was to come later, but rather in the portfolios of an obscure Scottish architect who was certainly unaware of just how his drawings would spur another Scot into changing the direction of English architecture. James Smith (c. 1645–1731) was eulogised by Colen Campbell in the second, 1717, volume of *Vitruvius Britannicus* as 'the most experienc'd Architect in that Kingdom'. To judge by Smith's executed work he was not a Palladian, for Hamilton Palace, Lanarkshire, of about 1697, is Anglo–French in style rather than Anglo–Italian. Palladianism, for Smith, was an entirely theoretical exercise upon Palladian themes, notably Palladio's Villa Rotonda (Fig. 31), his town houses such as the Vicentine Palazzo Iseppo di Porto, and, surprisingly, Webb's Gallery at Somerset House (Fig. 30). These exercises were almost certainly made when Smith 'went abroad to Italy and studied his Art' from about 1670 to 1675. Seen in this light they are not necessarily evidence of a neo-Palladian interest, but rather a Palladian one by the young Smith who was then closer to Jones and Webb in spirit than to the baroque Wren. Smith's exercises would have been quite unremarkable had his drawings not been acquired by a lawyer and architect to be, Colen Campbell, for it was this that led directly to the fountain-head of neo-Palladianism proper. With the canniness of his race, Campbell saw his main chance in Smith's portfolios and he had no hesitation in plundering them for ideas. What Smith thought of this we cannot tell, but Campbell was in any case too pre-occupied in proselytizing the new style to have cared very much.

The first truly neo-Palladian building of the new epoch can be precisely dated, for when William Benson (1682–1754) leased Amesbury Abbey in 1708 he almost immediately began to build himself a new house nearby, and he called it Wilbury (Fig. 33). Now there can be little doubt that this name was composed of the *Wil* of Wilton and the *bury* of Amesbury, commemorating two houses believed to be by Jones, for the elevation of Wilbury was no less than the top half of Amesbury laid upon the ground to a plan from Palladio. In 1708 then Benson is a champion of Jones. Not enough is known about this early period in either Benson's career or Campbell's for it to be possible to suggest that Benson was the catalyst in turning Campbell from a lawyer and amateur architect into a professional neo-Palladian. All we can say is that Campbell's church designs, submitted to the Commission for Building Fifty New Churches in 1711, could hardly be described as

Palladian, rather they are Wrennish. But they may well reflect Smith's style, for Smith must have been some sort of master to Campbell in Scotland. Benson certainly became Campbell's crony, and when Benson eventually ousted Wren from the Surveyorship of the Works in 1718, it was Campbell who became his Deputy. It would be interesting if Benson could be connected in any way with contemporary events in Oxford where Dr Henry Aldrich had designed the Peckwater Quadrangle at Christchurch in 1707. The elevations around three sides of a courtyard manifest a new spirit in English architecture, for each side is Jonesian in style, consisting of fifteen bays and one and a half storeys, divided by Ionic pilasters over a smooth rusticated basement, and with alternate segmental and triangular pediments. Peckwater's amazing classicality was a reflection of Aldrich's compilation of a learned and scholarly treatise, *Elementa Architecturae*, which, even if incomplete, nevertheless contained the first plans and elevations in an English book of villas and town houses by Palladio. Peckwater has more merit than has been accorded it, for not only do its elevations contain the germ of Wanstead derived from a design in Scamozzi, but in its architectural treatment of a basically compartmented terrace scheme, it is surely a model for urban facades in squares such as Queen's Square, Bath.

Another Oxford academic who must claim a place in the overture to the Palladian revival is Dr George Clarke who had acquired those drawings by Jones and Webb, with a few by Palladio, that had become detached from the Talman collection. Clarke's Palladian exercises after some of these designs secure him some claim to be a precursor in the revival, for his project of about 1710 for the new building at All Souls College, Oxford is an astonishing revival of Webb's project for rebuilding Cobham Hall, Kent, in 1638, and others are based upon one of his Belvoir projects. All this, however, may well have been contained within the city walls of Oxford, but Clarke did function albeit ineffectively, as one of the Church Commissioners, and a familiarity with Campbell may be borne out by Campbell's dedication to him of the plate of the Banqueting House in *Vitruvius Britannicus*, 1715. Quite clearly a favourable situation was developing during these crucial years around 1707 to 1712, a hint as to which is provided by John James in a letter to the Duke of Buckingham, in which he stated that the 'Beautys of Architecture may consist with the greatest plainess of the structure . . . (something that) has scarce even been hit on by the Tramontani unless by our famous Mr Inigo Jones'. Somehow Campbell was astute enough soon after 1711 to realise that his main chance as an architect lay with architectural reform.

Campbell's realisation was soon to be effected, for the first design for Wanstead House, Essex, is dated 1713, a year when he must have been preparing his material for engraving in *Vitruvius Britannicus*, first advertised in June 1714 and published in 1715. If anything marks the beginning of the Palladian revival it is this. A few months later the first instalment of Giacomo Leoni's edition of Palladio's *Quattro Libri* appeared, and this first full translation into English of all Palladio's books was another beacon that announced the new style. Campbell's championship of British architecture is at once apparent in his introduction in which he confesses that his collection of examples 'will admit of a fair Comparison with the best of the moderns' and by 'moderns' he meant the best of late 17th century French and Italian architecture. Despite those 'Restorers of Architecture', Bramante, Serlio, Scamozzi, etc, it was 'the great Palladio, who has exceeded all that were gone before him, and surpass'd his Contemporaries'. 'It is then', Campbell continues, 'with the Renowned Palladio we enter the Lists, to which we oppose the Famous Inigo Jones'. Basically Campbell's ploy in *Vitruvius Britannicus* was a subtle one designed to effect and propagandize a revolution in architectural taste, but in so doing to advance his own designs, beginning with his prophetic and austere Wanstead (Figs 35–7). He could not ignore such contemporaries as Sir John Vanbrugh, whose still unfinished Blenheim Palace, Oxfordshire, was included as one of the examples of national achievement; but Campbell could hope that Vanbrugh's baroque palace would be seen in contrast with the classicality of Wanstead and as we know from Vanbrugh's own Grimsthorpe Castle, Lincolnshire (Fig. 49) published in *Vitruvius Britannicus*, III, 1725, Vanbrugh was eventually obliged to bend with the prevailing wind. Apart from Wanstead, proffered in two designs, known to architectural history as Wanstead I and Wanstead II, Campbell inserted his own designs as a lure for patronage, such as the 'New Design of my own Invention in the Style of Inigo Jones' dedicated to the Duke of Argyll, an 'Iseppo di Porto' design dedicated to Lord Islay, and others to Lord Halifax and Lord Perceval. The Palladian derivation of all these is clear and the contrast with the restless compositions of Vanbrugh, Hawksmoor or Archer could not have been greater. Campbell had achieved a triumph, for he had demonstrated the way that British taste was to develop. From this first volume of *Vitruvius Britannicus* would emerge the 'national taste' that the Earl of Shaftesbury had, in a pamphlet published in 1712, wished to see formed. Confirmation as to the progress of events over two years was provided by *Vitruvius Britannicus* II in 1717 when Campbell presented two more new houses, for Sir Charles Hotham and John Hedworth, but he was still feeling his way, and it was not until *Vitruvius Britannicus* III in 1725 that the public was able to see engravings that displayed Campbell's mastery of the Palladian great house, the villa, and the town house. The great house was represented by the extended version of Wanstead (p. 17) and by Houghton Hall, Norfolk, 1722 (Fig. 38); the villa by Stourhead, Wiltshire (Fig. 40) of about 1720, with variations of the rotunda villa at Mereworth Castle, Kent (Fig. 42) about 1722; and the town house by Burlington House, Piccadilly (Fig. 46) of 1718, the Rolls House, Chancery Lane, 1717, and Pembroke House, Whitehall (Fig. 44) completed 1724.

In particular, although he may not have invented the astylar terrace that was to become a characteristic Georgian urban facade, he was

Engraving of Wanstead III from Colen Campbell's *Vitruvius Britannicus*. 1725

possibly the first in the 18th century to adopt it. There were even earlier precedents for the terrace with *piano nobile* than Peckwater, notably Jones's development in Lothbury for Lord Maltravers (if it was built according to the design). Associated with this aspect of urban facadism was the treatment of one side of a square behind a grid of the orders. Campbell proposed this for Grosvenor Square in 1725 (Fig. 45), but again Peckwater Quad looms as a source. Campbell's achievement was to provide easily copied models for a variety of neo-Palladian building types, and as his architecture was composed of simple identifiable elements derived from Palladio, Jones or Webb, and his secret portfolio of Smith's designs, it was easily copied. Even if we overlook the frankly plagiarist aspect of Campbell's methods, the total result was little less than remarkable considering it represented about ten years activity.

In that second volume of *Vitruvius Britannicus* published in 1717 the engraving of the Casina or Bagnio at Chiswick is inscribed by Campbell and dated 1717 as 'the first essay of His Lordship's happy invention', his lordship being Richard Boyle, 3rd Earl of Burlington and 4th Earl of Cork (1694–1753: see p. 19). Whether Burlington invented this or not matters little, for it is a perfectly Campbellian design resembling the facades of the end bays of Burlington House in Piccadilly, soon to be building to Campbell's designs. It was about this time that Burlington was inspired to study architecture. In 1719 whilst his town house was building he set off for Vicenza, and like Jones he purchased his Palladio in Venice and toured the Veneto with it in his hand. Again like Jones, he too made an astonishing coup, for in the stables of the Villa Maser he found all Palladio's drawings of Roman antiquity. The Villa had been the home of Palladio's great friend and patron Daniele Barbaro, editor of the 1556 Vitruvius for which Palladio had provided the plates. Spurred on by this, hardly had Burlington arrived back home (with, incidentally, William Kent) than William Talman died, an event that would lead after negotiations with Talman's son John to Burlington's purchase, in 1720 of all Jones's and Webb's designs, and in 1721 of all

Palladio's. These were to directly affect Burlington's method of composition and the creative outcome would justify Scipione Maffei's eulogy of him as 'il Palladio e il Jones de' nostri tempi'.

Just as Jones needed a few years to assimilate the implications of the second Italian voyage, so Burlington needed the testing ground of Tottenham Park, Wiltshire (Figs 50–52), built from 1720 for his brother-in-law Lord Bruce. Just possibly there is something in the make-up of this house that may reflect a first acquaintance with the Jones–Webb drawings, but essentially it was a text-book house drawing upon Palladio's *Four Books* and parts of Amesbury. Tottenham was the first neo-Palladian tower house with Venetian windows set in the tower fronts *à la* Wilton. So far there is no hint of those spatially complex rooms derived from antique Roman planning and Palladio's own designs and soon to be demonstrated at Chiswick. Then in 1722 Burlington scored a notable victory in the centre of London by wresting the design for the Westminster School Dormitory from Wren's man, William Dickenson. The facade (Fig. 53) is also untainted by original Palladian drawings, but it is Jonesian, for Burlington has ingeniously adapted the Covent Garden 'piazza' facades, stripping them of their orders, and rendering them into stone. Ornament is minimal and the effect is one of clinical severity. This severity, this austerity, this antique mien, are precisely the qualities that distinguish Burlington's architecture from that of his contemporaries, even William Kent.

With 1723 a watershed occurs in Burlington's way of composing, for he is now ready to use Palladio's own designs. From about 1718 the ground behind Burlington House was under development and possibly controlled by Burlington. Campbell had built his houses here, and in 1721 Giacomo Leoni had begun for Lord Clifton what was to become Queensbury House, a design from Webb's Somerset House Gallery. For General George Wade, Burlington selected from Palladio's designs an unexecuted facade for a town house, and made it the facade, not to a street, but to a courtyard. This might seem plagiarist, and it would have been for Campbell, but for Burlington it was rather a theory of imitation in which homage is paid to a great master. On the other hand perhaps General Wade made the choice himself, for he was a highly cultured connoisseur. Certainly this method of copying does not occur again in Burlington's professional career.

Burlington was involved in at least twenty six works, large and small, but central to them all is his own Chiswick Villa (Fig. 57). The story of Chiswick in the most simple terms is that Burlington had inherited a Jacobean house, and that from about 1715 the gardens were laid out, possibly by Charles Bridgeman, and that both James Gibbs and Campbell had been involved in placing temples as terminating points of straight avenues, something of a pioneering move in garden planning, and derivative from the theatre. Indeed, the theatric element is strong at Chiswick, not only in the *patte d'oie* to these avenues, regarded as a stage, but in the layout of the new orangery with its scenic topiary. From about 1720 Burlington himself took control and may have been entirely responsible for an area of new garden development comprising the amphitheatrical Orange Tree Garden with its domed rotunda temple and obelisk, and two shaped basons of water, one flanked by a Tuscan, Jonesian-like temple (Fig. 125). At the same time the old house was refronted (Fig. 58) with a narrow in-fill, refining upon the Bagnio but including for the first time in English architecture a Diocletian window, an element that was to become as common as the Palladian or Venetian window. This is a semi-circular opening with two upright mullions.

It was then with his new Villa at Chiswick that Burlington proved his intellectual superiority as architect over all his contemporaries. It was begun in 1725 or 1726 and what was achieved, in the structure by about 1729 and in the whole not until the later 1730s, was grammatically one of the most learned and meticulously assembled houses of the whole century. It is an immaculate synthesis of ancient and modern masters: ancient Roman planning in the shapes and sequences of rooms via the Baths and Palladio's own designs influenced from ancient planning; proportions and elemental relationships from Palladio's own designs and from two of Scamozzi's own seminal villas: Molini and Pisani; Roman decorations and ornament via Antoine Desgodetz's *Les Edifices Antiques de Rome* of 1682; and chimney-pieces and other ornamental parts from original drawings by Jones and Webb. In addition to all this, William Kent introduced into the interiors (Figs 148–50) his own idiosyncratic decoration that somehow warmed the chill of Burlington's scholarship. Chiswick is unique as a building, and is the jewel in the neo-Palladian crown. It is also important if seen as one of the results of Burlington's office organization. As a noble amateur he was not an executant. He would make the first design and would, for example, then instruct his draughtsman to 'draw this by tomorrow morning'. He gathered around him, living either at Burlington House or at Chiswick, a group of young assistant architects. First there was Henry Flitcroft, then Isaac Ware, then Stephen Wright, all of whom became important Palladian architects in their own right. There was also Henry Savile who seems to have been the permanent assistant and who as far as we know built nothing in his own right, and also Daniel Garrett who seems to have been the clerk of works in the field. William Kent stands apart, for his was a genius that matched Burlington's own, and his warm lovable nature made up of frivolity and fun was an anodyne to Burlington's austere, positive attitudes. All his life Kent lived with Burlington: his place in the Burlington household was a very special one, and there is no reason not to presume a close homosexual relationship.

The next step from being an assistant to Burlington was to become insinuated into the Office of Works, thereby contributing to and controlling government design. Flitcroft was made Clerk of the Works at Westminster, Whitehall and St James's in 1726; Ware was made Clerk Itinerant and Draughtsman in 1728; Garrett was a Labourer in Trust at Richmond New Lodge from 1727. 'Clerk' or 'labourer' may seem to us to be menial positions, but for the 18th century they were

Portrait of Lord Burlington by Jonathan Richardson c. 1718 showing the Casina at Chiswick in the background. Courtesy of The National Portrait Gallery.

not: they could carry considerable executive responsibility.

This is not by any means the whole story for neo-Palladianism spread from several epicentres, but the fact remains that the invention of neo-Palladianism as practised by architects of the second generation, as distinct from Campbell and Burlington representing the first generation, owes much to Burlington's practice between 1721 and 1731.

Burlington's ten years of creative activity culminated in two astonishing designs, the unexecuted Chichester Council House of about 1730 (Plate X, Fig. 62) and the York Assembly Rooms of 1731 (Figs 63–5). At Chichester he proposed a strictly utilitarian version of Palladio's Basilica at Vicenza, but so chaste that it could almost have been described as stripped classical. Burlington provided expensive and

cheap alternatives, both with superimposed arcaded fronts, the cheaper one with interpenetrating side bays and pediment, to a plan no larger than a grand temple. The expensive version continued the arcaded theme with Diocletian windows above, right along the side for 12 bays. For sheer fundamentalism there was nothing in contemporary European architecture like this. Sadly no plan survives, and it can only be deduced that the great room was two stories high lit by the Diocletian windows casting light downwards from a source that, for the spectator on the ground, would have been undisclosed. The alternative solution for the interior might have been a columnar one, for this was meted out at the York Assembly Rooms, which for Burlington is the culmination of all that he had striven for since Tottenham Park. The Assembly Rooms is a modern interpretation of an ancient festival hall, crossed with what Palladio called an Egyptian Hall. Here is incarnated, therefore, the ancient master in Vitruvius and the modern in Palladio. Burlington prefaced his hall with an ingenious screened facade whose starting point was the Roman temple of Bacchus, via Palladio, but spatially opened up by the insertion of columnar screens from the Baths of Diocletian. Significantly Burlington published a selection of Palladio's drawings after the Roman Baths as *Fabbriche Antiche disegnate da Andrea Palladio* in 1730.

With the completion of the Assembly Rooms William Kent entered the architectural lists. He had been painter and decorator, and now it was almost as if Burlington was ready to hand over the mantle to one who had been described as the 'proper priest' to Burlington's 'Apollo of the arts'. A comparison between Jones and Webb and Burlington and Kent is instructive, for it suggests that Kent may have been the only member of Burlington's entourage who fully understood the intellectual basis of his architecture.

The first major house in which Burlingtonian principles were enshrined was Lord Leicester's Holkham in Norfolk, conceived by Burlington, Kent and Leicester in consort between about 1730 and 1734. These four years are critical because during them Burlington took the decision to join the new villa at Chiswick to the old building, forming what is known as the Link Building. The advance and recession of wall surfaces, and the additive nature of parts, composed of niches and seen as part of a composition that at Chiswick was extended on one side by the villa itself, and on the other by the Summer Parlour, can be described as producing a staccato or concatenated effect. In theory, parts could be added or subtracted from the whole at will. This concatenation was produced at Holkham by the addition to the main house of four large pavilions. With Chiswick as the *locus classicus*, the style of concatenation became idiosyncratically neo-Palladian. Holkham was also a Palladian tower house, and when Burlington added wings to Tottenham Park in about 1736 (Fig. 51) he created another Holkham in Wiltshire. Burlington's works combined with Holkham provided all the fuel for neo-Palladian needs until the advent of neo-classicism, but Holkham had one other stroke of genius to offer in its great hall, a columnar invention sired by the antique as interpreted by Vitruvius and Palladio, but crossed by a modern work, Palladio's S Giorgio Maggiore with its intercolumniated choir, admired and published by Kent. It was a neo-Palladian reply to Jones's hall at Greenwich, and likewise its influence was profound, reverberating in museums, hotels and assembly rooms until the present day.

The great partnership between Apollo and his priest would have been triumphantly proclaimed had their new Houses of Parliament been built. All that survives is an astonishing sequence of designs (Fig. 70) that if published might have exerted a considerable influence on European architecture. They have not a little spice of later French *Grand Prix* exercises, and in spirit such designs as that for the House of Commons (Plate I) would not have looked out of place in Revolutionary Paris. The problem of disentangling Burlington and Kent in these works is as intractable as that of Jones and Webb with the Whitehall designs. The antique and modern authority behind them is undisputed, and their grammar had already been collected when William Kent published in 1727 *The Designs of Inigo Jones, with some Additional Designs* (by Burlington and himself). In these two volumes Kent published many of the designs by Jones and Webb as well as one of the Whitehall projects, and this project, more than any other, became the great quarry for neo-Palladian architects and builders, as well as pattern book compilers, seeking approved models for windows, doorways, parts of facades, and ornamental details. Although *Vitruvius Britannicus* was in effect a pattern book of national architecture, it was never quarried to the same extent as Kent's and in particular this applies to the disputed project for Whitehall Palace (known as the 'C' scheme) published in *Vitruvius Britannicus* II, 1717, which may not even be of Webb's time, although if from Wren's period of Surveyorship it would have considerable neo-Palladian significance.

The increase in architectural publications in England between 1715 and, say, 1775 was an entirely English phenomenon: nowhere else in the world were so many books published. These books, more than any other event, determined the spread of the Campbellian and Burlingtonian gospel throughout the provinces. The rise of the pattern book as an educative tool has been shown in the case of Batty Langley to be masonic, and all Langley's books, both large and small, were meant to teach bricklayers, builders and architects the rules of building. William Halfpenny's *Magnum in Parvo* in 1722, or *Practical Architecture* in 1724, or the *Art of Sound Building* in 1725, ensured that the country builder could obtain access to reasonably-priced pattern books that would enable him to design an elevation with correct windows and doorways, or a room with well proportioned panelling and a Palladian chimney-piece. In *Practical Architecture*, for example, there is a 'Table of Proportions Calculated from the Door of Inigo Jones; or 'A Rustick Door from Palladio', or a 'Window taken from the Venetians'. Naturally, quality varied according to the capacity of the builder, and no doubt Jones would have been horrified to see what the likes of

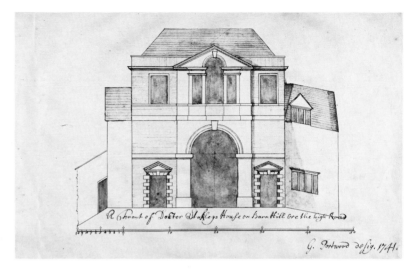

George Portwood's unexecuted design for rebuilding Dr William Stukeley's house on Barn Hill, Stamford, Lincolnshire, 1741

George Portwood might do to his Palladian and voussoired windows in a house in Stamford, Lincolnshire (see p. 20). In many ways Palladian or neo-Palladian is a misnomer for much of the style of building in our county and cathedral towns, and perhaps it is better to simply call it Georgian, but nevertheless, even if derived at secondhand from pattern books, it must be admitted that its hero ought to be Webb rather than Jones.

The Palladian revival spread from 1715 and weakens as a clear stylistic statement in the 1750s, although neo-Palladian buildings continued to appear in the provinces, and especially in Ireland and Scotland as late as 1800. There is also the question of the twin streams of neo-Palladianism and neoclassicism meeting in architects such as William Chambers and Robert Adam, the former relying upon villa models for his country houses, the latter attracted by the plastic shapes of Burlington's Chiswick rooms and neo-Palladian wall elements. The 1750s was also the decade of Strawberry Hill and the Gothick (with a k) revival, and it may come as a surprise to some that a neo-Palladian architect such as William Kent could regard Gothick as an admissible alternative. During the period under examination Gothick was always used as an associational style, for additions to earlier buildings. Hence Kent added to Hampton Court in 1732, or to Wolsey's old Tudor tower at Esher Place in 1733. He thereby enlarged it into one of the seminal rococo-gothic houses of the whole pre-Strawberry Hill era. Kent's Esher became to Georgian Gothick what Burlington's Chiswick had been to neo-Palladianism. In the same spirit was Hawksmoor's completion of the west towers of Westminster Abbey in 1734 and his additions to the 14th century Knights of the Garter stalls there. His project for Honingham Hall, Norfolk in 1737 (Fig. 71) is entirely characteristic of his charming and insouciant Gothick, and it was almost to be a blue-print for what he would do at Rousham House, Oxfordshire, the following year.

An 'office' whether it be under Burlington's supervision, or in the Board of Works, not only produces a common style of building but one of architectural draughtsmanship and calligraphy too. It is often tediously difficult to distinguish between the drafting style of Flitcroft or Ware, and the same can be said of Kent and Vardy. Vardy first appears as Clerk of Works at Greenwich in 1736 and he was probably Kent's executive and clerk of works throughout the 1730s and indeed until Kent died in 1748. He completed Kent's Horse-Guards at Whitehall (Holkham brought to town) and in 1744 had published *Some Designs of Mr Inigo Jones and Mr William Kent*, the picture book that was to disseminate true Kentian Gothick. Vardy's alternative stylistic solutions for Milton Abbey, Dorset of the 1750s (Fig. 72) could hardly be closer both in draughtsmanship and architectural style to Kent.

The architects who hand down emulative country house models are Campbell and Burlington, not Kent, whose only completed classical country house was Frederick, Prince of Wales's, Palace at Kew, begun in 1730. (Wakefield Lodge, Northamptonshire, was built after Kent's death.) There were, however, others on the fringe of Burlington's patronage who established an influential neo-Palladian practice. One such was Giacomo Leoni (*c.* 1686–1746). Just as Leoni could claim a first with his edition of Palladio in 1715, so in the third volume of *The Architecture of L.B. Alberti* in 1726 he was one of the first architects to publish a special corpus of his own work (see p. 21). Kent followed in 1727 and James Gibbs with his *Book of Architecture* in 1728. Leoni tended to fluctuate between large but somewhat austere brick houses and huge swaggering designs like Carshalton Park, Surrey begun about 1723 but never finished. Like many of Leoni's works which display an element of bravado Carshalton is tainted with a feeling of baroque plasticity and this same tendency permeates the redrawing of plates in the Palladio. Leoni, in other words, was not a dedicated neo-Palladian and as far as Burlington was concerned was never allowed to penetrate much further than the courtyard of Burlington House. There were many other partial converts who still owed allegiance to the baroque, either through direct involvement, or, as with James Gibbs, coming from a training in Italy, in his case under Carlo Fontana and so in the ambience of the Roman Baroque. In one sense Gibbs is much the trimmer, steering a course between the extremes of the old and the new. As in his designs for Lowther Castle, Westmorland, about 1725 (Fig. 48), made in competition with Campbell, the surface treatment has a brio that Campbell's works never possess even when he too uses massively voussoired or rusticated openings.

In view of the spread of Palladianism throughout Ireland, which as a style was entirely imported, there is also Sir Edward Lovett Pearce (*c.* 1699–1733) to account for. He stands as a peer with Burlington and Kent, but his loyalties were first with Vanbrugh, to whom he was related and for whom he worked. Between 1723 and 1724 he amply

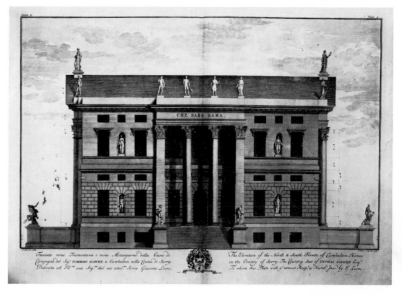

Giacomo Leoni's engraved elevation for the side of Carshalton Park, Surrey, begun for Sir Thomas Scawen in 1723. Published in Leoni's edition of *Alberti*, 1726 where the plates of Carshalton, however, are dated 1728

annotated his Palladio in the Veneto and by 1726 was established in Ireland. Soon after 1727 he sent over to London his designs for a palace for George II at Richmond (see p. 22) and with these would have excelled Campbell at his own game. Passages of columnar planning and the articulation of the facades reveal his Vanbrughian sympathies, but this would have been a remarkable neo-Palladian palace. Like Gibbs he too could not eradicate his baroque tendencies, and his designs for houses (Figs 105–6) have a liveliness that certainly makes them attractive, and in this he is perhaps closer to Kent. He virtually founded Irish Palladianism and within the half a dozen years before his death set down on Irish soil a series of magistrial buildings, including the Irish Parliament House. In 1729 he handed on his mantle to Richard Castle, the doyen of Irish Palladian architects.

Despite the overwhelming influence of the Burlington–Kent partnership as one of the twin vortices with Colen Campbell, neo-Palladianism became too common a language ever to retain the same integrity and discipline that was brought to their works by these three first-generation architects. In truth Burlington's assistants lacked creative genius. Daniel Garrett (died 1753), for example, may have built up a large northern practice, but as his designs for Kirtlington Park, Oxfordshire (see p. 22) demonstrate he was a competent but dull architect, livelier perhaps in the designing of Gothick temples. Of Henry Savile's own works nothing is known. Stephen Wright (died 1780) spent most of his life as a member of the Board of Works, but he enjoyed the Duke of Newcastle's patronage, and it was through the Duke that he designed the exquisite University Library at Cambridge in 1754, a

Kentian elevation laced with rococo that may hint that Wright did more than we can credit him for. Even Henry Flitcroft (1697–1769) with major houses such as Wentworth Woodhouse, Yorkshire, from 1735 and Woburn Abbey, Bedfordshire, 1747, hardly rises to dazzling brilliance. Wentworth is gigantic but monotonous in composition, an essay on Wanstead III, and Woburn is frankly derivative from John Sanderson's Stratton Park, Hampshire of 1731. More than any other architect, Flitcroft adheres to a Jonesian canon made up from Campbell, the Whitehall designs in *Vitruvius Britannicus* and Kent's books. He is better as the master of the elegant Palladian interior, specialising in attractive permutations of Jonesian chimney-piece designs. He could, for example, have designed the Somerset House chimney-pieces that are attributed to Kent (Fig. 152). He has not yet been given his rightful due as an architect of temples in parkscapes, for those at Stourhead are by him and possibly even the Temple of Concord at Stowe. He was responsible for laying out Windsor Great Park for the Duke of Cumberland in the middle 1740s. His building most familiar to the public is, of course, the church of St Giles in the Fields (Figs 79–84), 1731–1734, which relied on the plans for Wren's city churches and James Gibbs's St Martins in the Fields. It is frankly not original, but the nave is wrapped round with authoritative neo-Palladian details.

It is conceivable that a close working relationship with Burlington did not create conditions for great originality, that Isaac Ware (died 1766) and Roger Morris (1659–1749), whose subservience to Burlington is disputed, should be seen as two second-generation architects who, therefore, rise above the common run of their colleagues for originality and independence. They both exercised great influence because of their dominant country house practice; both built town houses as well and it was Morris, for example, who actually designed the Council House at Chichester in 1731. Morris proves himself the undisputed master of the neo-Palladian villa with models (such as Combe Bank, Kent (Figs 73–7) of about 1725, Westcombe House, Blackheath, about 1730 and Whitton Place, Middlesex, about 1732) nearly always small in scale and exquisite in execution. Morris was particularly sensitive to the relationship of the main block to the subsidiary offices, often creating an interplay of cubic forms. Morris's allegiances are first to Campbell, for whom he acted in the 1720s as an executant, then to Lord Pembroke as a close architectural confidant and amanuensis. But he was also involved in many commissions with Lord Burlington, for he, Burlington and Pembroke designed that splendid Palladian house at Castle Hill, Devon, from 1729 and Kirby Hall, Yorkshire was built to his and Burlington's designs in 1747.

Ware's houses are different in style, his vocabulary wider and more eclectic, and he was receptive to the emerging rococo of the 1740s. His Wrotham Park, Middlesex, of 1754, is a reduction of the third design for Wanstead, in effect, converting the great house into the extended villa. All Ware's work has great chic and expresses supreme confidence. The

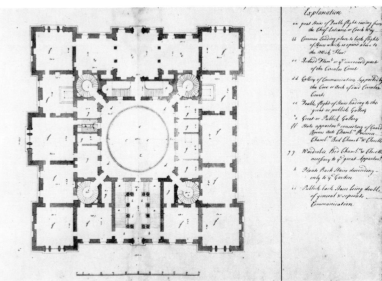

Top and centre: Sir Edward Lovett Pearce's plan and elevation for a royal palace at Richmond Gardens, Surrey, proposed for George II soon after 1727 but never built. *Courtesy Sir Richard Proby, Elton Hall*

Bottom: Daniel Garrett's unexecuted design for rebuilding Kirtlington Park, Oxfordshire, for Sir James Dashwood, 1751. *Private Collection*

loss of such stunning houses as Amisfield, East Lothian (see p. 37) built in 1756 and demolished in 1928 must be bitterly regretted. His translation of Palladio's *Four Books of Architecture* in 1738 was an impeccable job, as was the redrawing of the plates. It was dedicated to Lord Burlington, and its correctness is reflected in all Ware's works through the 1730s. Burlington, for example, would have approved of the lineage of Ware's submission for the rebuilding of the Mansion House in 1735 (see p. 23). When Amisfield was built, Burlington was dead, and no doubt its interiors were already rococo-tinctured, for this was the very year that Ware published his *Complete Body of Architecture*, a massive compendium of Georgian design that already reveals the dissolution of those neo-Palladian disciplines that were accepted without dissent until the 1740s. It was, in fact, the great *magnum in parvo* and with it the architect could achieve miracles for his client.

After the 1740s Georgian Palladianism, which is a style very distant from the true Palladio and Jones, washes over the provinces. Nearly always between second-generation neo-Palladianism in metropolitan centres and the country executant, there is the pattern book. Masses of designs and buildings can barely be described as Palladian. Even a compiler such as William Halfpenny could only produce designs (Fig. 102) that have a rustic charm. If windows and doors (Fig. 104) derive from Webb's Whitehall designs, the body of the building bears little relationship to any model by Jones, Webb, Campbell or Burlington. This is not to denigrate the Halfpennys of the provinces, for their contribution to the Georgian well-being of our cathedral and market towns was visually rewarding, but is rarely Palladian. In certain towns architect-families established an identifiable 'office' or family style and William (1712–1776), David (died 1758) and Francis (1744–1789) Hiorne (or Hiorns) of Warwick are typical of many. Such county architects (and there was Pritchard of Shrewsbury or Portwood of Stamford) often changed the stylistic character of their towns and villages. William and David Hiornes' Gopsall Hall, Leicestershire (Figs 98–99) was one of their bigger country house jobs and really all that survives of neo-Palladian endeavour are elements like Palladian windows, or a grand classical portico. The interiors were frankly a mish-mash of fairly exuberant rococo decoration by plasterers who clearly worked without control. Naturally there were exceptional centres, and Bath was one, and there John Wood the elder (1704–1754) could, if he had wished, have acquired a metropolitan reputation equivalent to a Flitcroft or a Ware. In fact he began his career in London and seems to have belonged to the circle of Harley, Earl of Oxford, that included James Gibbs. Perhaps he saw Gibbs as a competitor and moved to Bath where he contributed to the first major phase of urban development in that city. On the whole his designs are reserved in elevation and he became a master of the astylar street front (Fig. 108) and in Prior Park, outside Bath, produced his version of Wanstead I.

Matthew Brettingham (1699–1769) was another county architect, this time in Norfolk, who had learnt his trade building Holkham. He spread

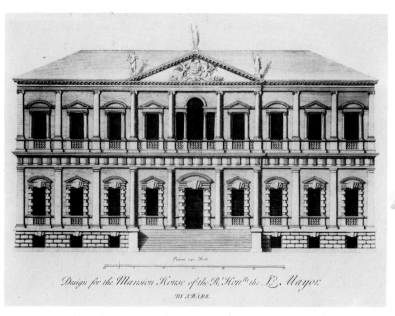

Isaac Ware's engraved elevation for his Mansion House, London, competition of 1735

the neo-Palladian gospel throughout East Anglia, and then through his activities spilled over into the Midlands and then to London where he seems to have become the fashionable architect for handsome but plain town houses. In elevation these are usually old-fashioned and slightly gauche, and nearly all of them boast a Venetian window either lighting the staircase from the front or back. He might have become the architect of Lord Leicester's town house in Berkeley Square had it been built. His designs (Figs 93–4) show various permutations of the placement of elements and his rooms are nearly all square in shape with perhaps a columnar episode in a hall or to the stairs. Brettingham could have been the architect of the designs (Figs 85–91) for Cholmondeley House, perhaps in Whitehall, London, which demonstrate how a patron would be presented with a full set of plans, elevations, sections; designs for ceilings and chimney-pieces, for the stables, and even directions for hanging the pictures (Fig. 92). In contrast to Leicester House, Cholmondeley was of moderate expense and might have cost between £6,000 and £8,000 in the 1750s. It is instructive to compare both the Leicester and Cholmondeley designs with a set by Lord Burlington, in this case (Figs 66–9) for the 2nd Duke of Richmond's town house in Whitehall submitted in 1730. Here, in contrast, is a tautly disciplined design, not only thought-out, but drawn out with confidence, and with every detail acknowledging Palladio, Jones, Webb or antique Rome. One other neo-Palladian architect demands attention because a large corpus of designs by him survive, but comparitively little is known about

continued on page 37

23

List of colour plates

I. William Kent's laid-out wall plan design for the House of Commons drawn January 23, 1735. Pen and watercolour (480 × 460)

II. John Sanderson's sectional design for a circular domed rotunda in a country house, possibly for Copped Hall, Essex, about 1753. Pen and watercolour (425 × 250)

III. William Kent's sectional design for a neo-Palladian hall drawn as plate 68 for his *Inigo Jones* in 1727 and intended for an unlocated situation. Pen and wash (360 × 490)

IV. John Sanderson's laid-out wall plan design for the saloon at Kimberley Park, Norfolk, presented to Sir Armine Wodehouse in 1761. Pen and wash (480 × 560)

V. John Vardy's laid-out wall plan design for a room at Milton Abbey in Dorset possibly in the 1760s and combining rococo ornament with pilasters based upon those in a room at The Queen's House. Pen, pencil and wash (370 × 470)

VI. James Paine's laid-out wall plan design for the Dining Room at Gopsall Hall, Leicestershire, 1764, but not executed. Here Paine has translated the Kentian architectonic interior into a more rococo idiom. Pen and wash (525 × 370)

VII. William Hiorne's design for the Summer House fronting the Bowling Green at Gopsall Hall, Leicestershire, about the 1750s. Pen and wash (315 × 545)

VIII. A sheet of studies for neo-Palladian villas made by Matthew Brettingham the younger (1725–1803) when travelling through Italy in 1747. Pen and wash (265 × 200)

IX. Design for the west portico of the church of St Martins in the Fields, London by Sir James Thornhill (1675–1734) submitted on 20 July 1720 when he attended the Committee of Commissioners for rebuilding. Pen and wash (520 × 395)

X. Lord Burlington's side elevation for the Council House at Chichester, Sussex, about 1730. Pen and wash (290 × 445)

XI. Inigo Jones's astylar elevational design for the Prince's Lodging at Newmarket Palace, Cambridgeshire, about 1619. Pen and watercolour (185 × 275)

XII. The Banqueting House in Whitehall viewed by a Victorian watercolourist renderer, who has added statues to the balustrade. Watercolour (580 × 900)

January yᵉ 23 1735
the King came to yᵉ house of Lords
to other a speaker for yᵉ house
of commons mʳ onnslow was
at yᵉ Barr & yᵉ Black rod stood by him

Duke of Bolton held yᵉ cap of mentenance
Lord ownsly yᵉ sword of state
Duke montague & Duke of Richmond
Duke of Ancaster Lord great chamberlaine with his rod

prince of wales

III

A Section for the Saloon at Kimberly near Wyndham in Norfolk
Sec.r S.r Armine Wodehouse Bar.t The Walls to be plain Stucco
on Lath, ornamented with medallions & Bas relief heads
and the festoons to be Stucco or Pipe Masticc

IV

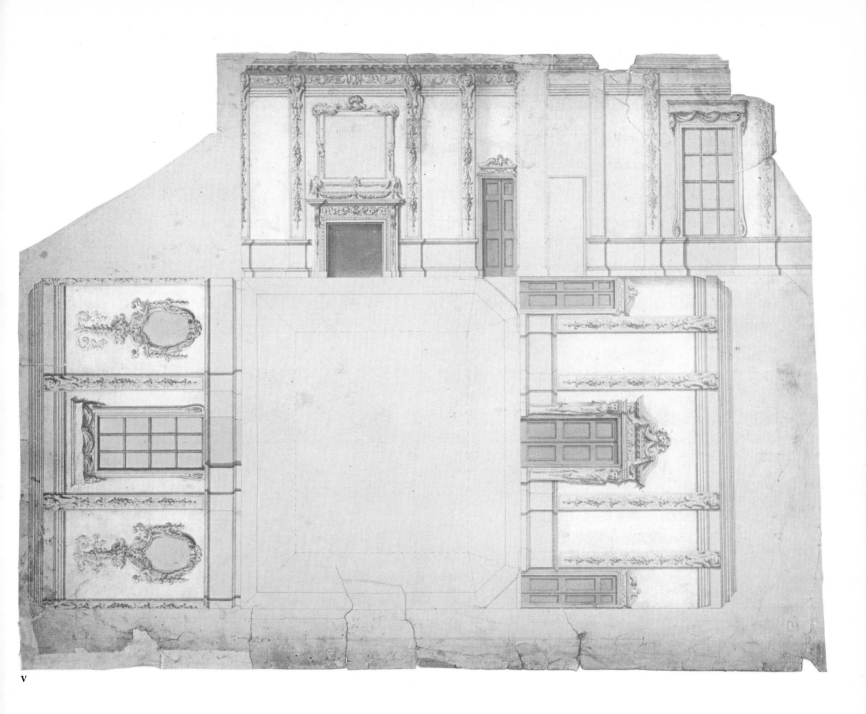

V

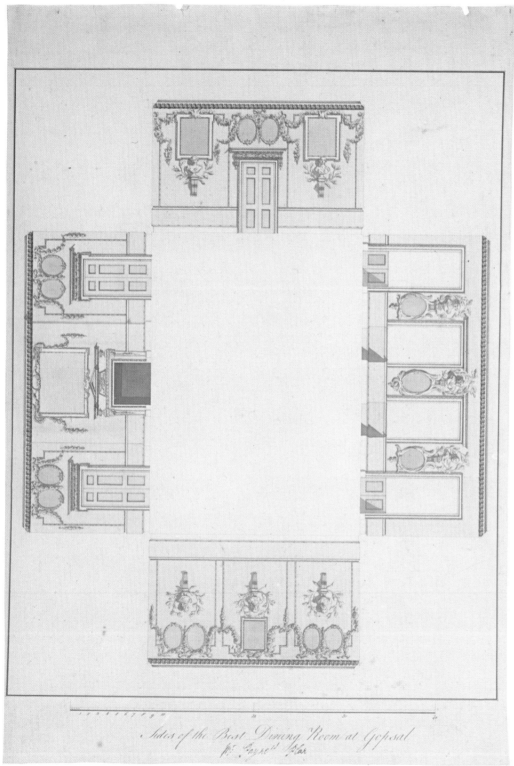

Sides of the Best Dining Room at Gopsal

VI
30

VII

31

For St. Martins Church.

IX

A Draught of the Earl of Burlingtons,
for the the front of a Councill house
for the Corporation of Chichester.

X

34

XI

XII

Amisfield House, East Lothian, Scotland, photographed 1883, demolished in 1928. Built by Isaac Ware for Francis Charteris 1756

the extent of his practice. John Sanderson (died 1774) had built two huge Palladian houses by 1731: Kelham Hall, Nottingham and Stratton Park, Hampshire, so he may well be of first-generation vintage, living to a great age. He was a draughtsman of exquisite skill (Plate II), much above the common run, and his designs comprise many for first-rate buildings (Figs 96–7) including a set of working drawings for a rotunda type villa that may have been built, but the location for which is now lost.

The lot of most professional architects was to be conditioned by precedent, which was of itself a corollary of the dictates of fashion. There was, however, one group of architects who by virtue of their special position, usually of the landed classes, could afford to be untrammelled. These were amateurs for whom architecture was either a hobby, or was a secondary occupation. They were not by any means noblemen of the Burlington or Pembroke class, but often men of business. The desire to design for themselves or for others cuts right through the social strata, and no doubt many a country parsonage was designed by the incumbent. Some amateurs had great reputations but have been forgotten. Such a one was Sir Andrew Fountaine of Narford in Norfolk, whom Robert Morris regarded as forming a triumvirate with Burlington and Pembroke, but all that visually survives to credit him with is the glimpse, in an engraving, of an austere Burlingtonian facade to the library wing of his house said to have been added as early as 1718, and so pre-Burlingtonian. In fact the surface treatment compares with the chasteness of the Westminster Dormitory facade.

The third member of the triumvirate, Henry Herbert, 9th Earl of

Pembroke (c. 1689–1750) can be credited with many splendid neo-Palladian buildings, but no securely documented design in his hand survives for any of them, so the actual processes of conveying the design to the executant is unknown. Roger Morris was involved in nearly all his works, and certainly must have come to Pembroke via Campbell, who had designed Pembroke's house in Whitehall in about 1723 and on which Morris worked. Pembroke and Morris are credited with Marble Hill, Twickenham, 1724, the White Lodge in Richmond New Park, 1727, Wimbledon House, Surrey, 1732, as well as the exquisite Palladian Bridge at his lordship's own Wilton in Wiltshire, in 1736. Possibly Pembroke's is the drawing or design for the little Water House at Houghton Hall, Norfolk (see p. 40) built about 1730, which is the centre section of his Whitehall house. Pembroke must have been able to draw for there would be no other way by which to convey detailed instructions. It is simply that as most of his private papers have disappeared, so have his drawings. The frequency of the collaborative job is perhaps underestimated. A good example of this on a grand scale is Castle Hill, Devon, remodelled for Lord Clinton from 1729 with Morris executing the contracts, and both Lords Pembroke and Burlington giving directions. It would be fascinating to know if the idiosyncrasies in Morris's work, notably in his villa models, were due to Pembroke's amateur status.

At the other end of the scale Theodore Jacobsen (died 1772) could be singled out as the successful city merchant who carried on a busy practice, again employing executants. Jacobsen's best known works are the Foundling Hospital in London, 1742–52, with utilitarian elevations, followed by Trinity College, Dublin, from 1752. Had Jacobsen's design for a Bank of England been accepted and executed (see p. 38), city finances would have been managed from a correct neo-Palladian villa.

The extent of amateur intervention in neo-Palladian affairs can only be estimated from existing documents, and sometimes these may be entirely theoretical. None of the drawings (Fig. 119) of Robert Hampden Trevor, Viscount Hampden (1706–1783) can be tied to any building. As a latinist and a scholar of refined taste, architectural drawing may have been a therapeutic exercise, with no obvious neo-Palladian family house to show for his efforts. Apart from Lord Burlington the most notable amateur architect of his own house was Sir Thomas Robinson (c. 1702–1777) whose Rokeby, Yorkshire (see p. 39) of about 1735 stands as an intellectual composition next to Chiswick for innovation in both planning and composition, but again there must have been some form of executant process, and in his case it may be significant that Isaac Ware not only drew out the Rokeby designs for engraving, but made many other drawings obviously intended for a treatise on Robinson's architecture. Another house amateur was Ambrose Phillips (c. 1707–1737), who had he not died so young might well have come to be noted in architectural annals. His travels through Italy and France soon after 1729 produced a group of

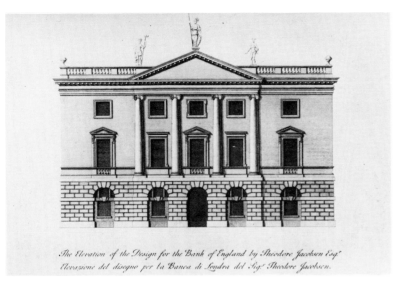

The Elevation of the Design for the Bank of England by Theodore Jacobsen Esq.
Elevazione del disegno per la Banca di Londra del Sig.^r Theodore Jacobsen.

Theodore Jacobsen's unexecuted plan and elevation for a new Bank of England, *c.* 1732, engraved by Fourdrinier

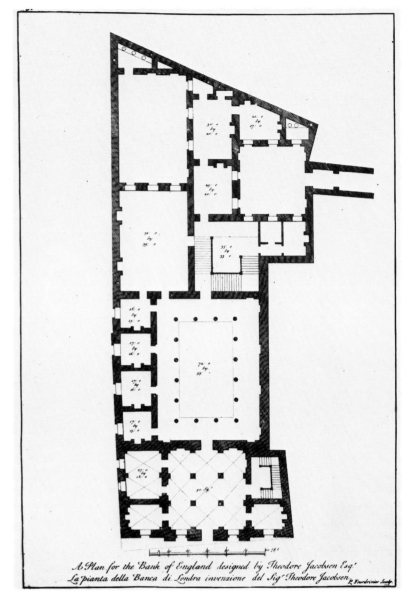

A Plan for the Bank of England designed by Theodore Jacobsen Esqr
La pianta della Banca di Londra invenzione del Sig.^r Theodore Jacobsen.

designs that are rare for their date in relying upon antique Roman sources in Provence. These were combined with neo-Palladian ones to produce an extraordinary project for the Place Royale du Peyrou at Montpellier (Figs 116–17), which being unexecuted, Phillips then used the flanking wings as the facade of his own house at Gardenon in Leicestershire. Phillips was one of the founding members of the Society of Dilettanti in 1734, as was Sir George Gray (died 1773), who was closely involved with John Vardy in the building of Spencer House in London, but whose only architectural design is for Palladian gate-piers at Caversham Park, Oxfordshire (Fig. 118). Finally it is worth mentioning Thomas Worsley (*c.* 1710–1778) who acquired the political sinecure in 1760 of Surveyor of the Office of Works. He was a most excellent neo-Palladian to judge by his own house at Hovingham Hall, Yorkshire (see p. 39) rebuilt from the 1750s and not a spice uninfluenced by his own officers in the Works, notably Vardy and Wright. Hovingham stands apart from precedent because Worsley ingeniously planned the domestic quarters around the menage and stables.

By virtue of his sinecure, and also it is worth adding, his large collection of architectural designs made by his officers, Worsley might be regarded as a quasi-professional, or at least a professional *manqué*. There were others like him, and the most interesting of these was Thomas Wright (1711–1786), a mathematician and astronomer who spent his whole life peripatetic from one noble household to another. He designed large and small houses, interiors, garden buildings and gardens, and like the amateur, always requiring the executant. His Nuthall Temple, Nottinghamshire (see p. 40) of 1754 is a Palladian rotunda villa that for sheer accomplishment and excellence stands third in the sequence Chiswick, Mereworth, Nuthall, Foots Cray, and for invention it is a better villa than Mereworth which is too closely modelled on the Villa Rotonda itself. Wright was associated with Kent, and this has sometimes led to confusion between him and Stephen Wright, and indeed, where Stephen built for Newcastle at Oatlands, Surrey, so Thomas laid out the great terrace there. Like Kent too he never made ruled drawings that could serve as a contractual basis for a builder. Wright was a true amateur in a particular social stratum that would have included the ecclesiastic. The amateur intervention is not, of course, only a by-product of neo-Palladianism. There were

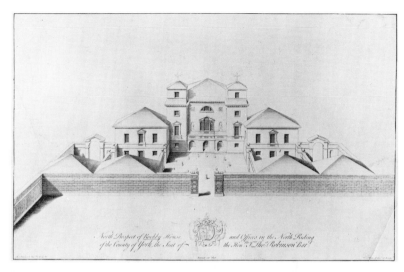

Sir Thomas Robinson's engraved perspective for rebuilding his own house at Rokeby, Yorkshire, *c.* 1730s, drawn and engraved by Isaac Ware

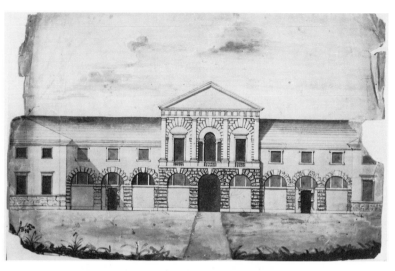

Thomas Worsley. Elevational perspective for rebuilding his own house at Hovingham Hall, Yorkshire, 1750s. *Courtesy Worsley Coll.*

Elizabethan courtiers who were amateurs; Wren came to architecture from science; Talman became the architect of the Williamite court from being a country gentleman, and such amateur activity occurs in the nineteenth century. However, it flourished strongest in the age of neo-Palladianism, when the landed gentry were living introspectively upon their estates, and estate management, in particular the uses of estate buildings, was of interest to nearly all owners. It is worth remembering that Daniel Garrett was the first architect to publish a book of such designs: *Designs and Estimates of Farm Houses*, 1747. Neo-Palladianism in these terms is difficult to compare with what was happening in other countries, but the amateur intervention in England at this time does appear to be a special phenomenon, and in many ways is one of the most satisfactory and interesting aspects of neo-Palladianism as a whole.

Apart from a few designs right at the very beginning of his architectural career, there is no drawing evidence that Jones concerned himself with those buildings subsidiary to the main one: stables, brew house, offices and perhaps farm buildings when the farm was attached to the house as it frequently was. The Newmarket Brew House (Fig. 121) and stable are therefore early, and after about 1619 Jones left such commissions to his subordinates. To accord with the utilitarian nature of these buildings, and following the authority of the Renaissance treatises, the Newmarket stable is primitively treated with rustics, and the brew-house is provided with a Scamozzian Tuscan order. A few designs by Webb survive and if he ever contemplated this class of design for his proposed treatise, he never progressed far. He was, however, the first professional architect to make a design for an architecturally ordered complex of farm house with farm buildings as a theoretical exercise.

Secondary and subsidiary buildings come into their own with neo-Palladianism, a fact that cannot be disassociated from the breaking down of the garden walls and the extension of the garden into the park. As garden systems were extended outwards, so those parts of the park that had hitherto been out of sight, were brought into view, and 'distant offices' in the case of Goodwood in 1724 (Fig. 128) required architectural treatment or adornment. The temple in the garden was one of the neo-Palladian ideals, even if Sir John Vanbrugh had already (by about 1715) begun to plant temples in his landscapes. As with so much else, Chiswick is a *locus classicus* in this, for there by about 1716 temples had been made into terminating points of *allées* or avenues, and barely five years later Burlington was to create the famous scene of water, Tuscan pavilion (Fig. 125) and the amphitheatrical orange tree garden. Campbell's role in all this is still unclear, but by 1724 Hall Barn in Buckinghamshire has been laid out with canals and terminating temple and rides with temples on axes, all loosely knit together. The number of temple designs (Figs 122–3) that survive in Campbell's collection show how concerned he was with this building type. During the period of neo-Palladianism of this first generation the temple idea seems usually to belong to a programme that might be either dictated by the architect or gardener. In other words, there is control. But like the force of neo-Palladianism in general, after the 1740s there is dissolution and the impression of visiting many of the parks laid out after this date is that temples or garden buildings are merely set down as eye-catchers in a position of visual appeal. A Capability Brown might have imposed a coherent plan upon a park, but usually in most cases the reason for the site of a temple was entirely visual and sometimes quite arbitrary. There are more garden buildings in England than in any other country, and the Gopsall collection shows (Figs 130–1) how stables, greenhouses, temples, bowling greens, all come within the province of the architect.

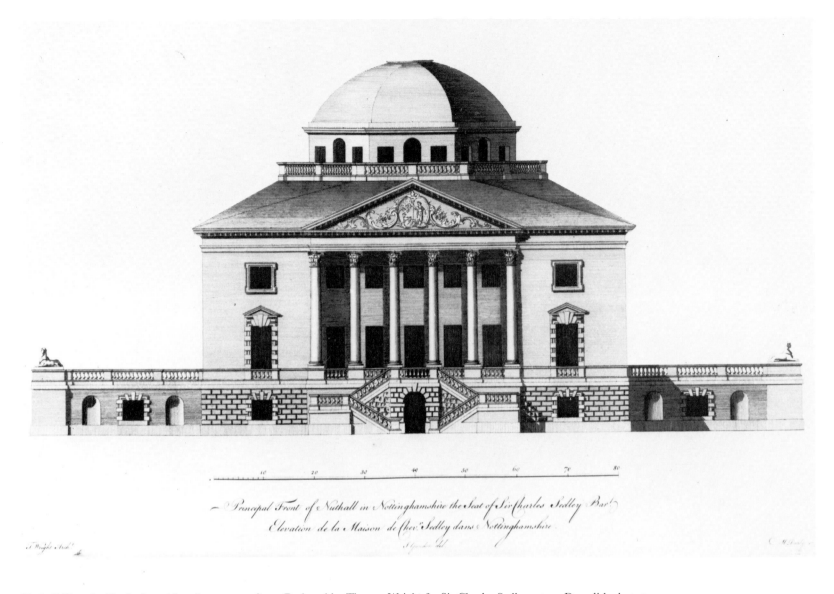

Principal Front of Nuthall in Nottinghamshire the Seat of Sir Charles Sedley Bart

Elevation de la Maison de Cher. Sedley dans Nottinghamshire

Nuthall Temple, Nottinghamshire, the entrance front. Designed by Thomas Wright for Sir Charles Sedley, 1754. Demolished 1929

There is also another aspect of the design of secondary and garden buildings. The small scale nature of their design made them more satisfactory for the provincial architect's endeavours. An Esau Reynolds (of Trowbridge, Wiltshire) might have built second-rate houses, but in the small compass of a gateway (Fig. 132) he could achieve something respectable. Often too, small scale buildings are the most attractive products of great architects, witness Jones's fertile designs for gateways (Figs 9–12), or Burlington's (Fig. 133), and when the latter made designs for small houses, as at Round Coppice, Buckinghamshire (Fig. 124), in 1727, the result is a *petite* masterpiece that we would all like to live in.

Jones's authority for decoration is almost entirely from Palladio and Serlio, but, as the years progress through the 1630s, with increasing divergences due to eclecticism. In the earlier works (and there is nothing surviving either in drawings or buildings before the Banqueting House of 1619) the decoration is archaeologising, from Roman antiquity as presented in Palladio's fourth book. For example, the barrel-vault of the St James's Chapel (Fig. 136) is based on the coffering of the Temple of Venus and Rome, and the ornamentation of the beams with *guilloche* in the Banqueting House comes from the same source, although it is quite a different matter as far as the compartmentation of the ceiling is concerned. For the barrel-vault in the House of Lords of 1623, however, Jones turned to the fourth book of Serlio, not so authoritative, but a richer quarry. Ceiling and wall decoration proved less of a problem to invent than the chimney-piece, a quintessential northern element. Serlio published a few, but for the St James's Chapel gallery Jones turned to his Scamozzi, choosing the Venetian *nappa*, that is the lower part that would support a mantel, and in the case of St James's, an overmantel. For overmantels there are many French precedents, and Jones must have known some of these, but the St James's one seems fanciful, and it is precisely the element of fancy that enters into Jones's grammar, a fancy not unassociated with Jones's masques designs and the great depth of experience that he had had in copying the Bolognese masters such as Parmigianino. From the time of the Somerset House Chapel onwards, generally through the 1630s, French decorative influences grow stronger, partly due to Queen Henrietta Maria introducing her own French decorators, whose designs Jones was compelled to redraw, and partly from Jones's fascination with French chimney-piece compilers such as Jean Barbet, whose book was published in 1633. John Webb hardly deviates from these same sources, in Palladio, Serlio and French ornament books, and his ceiling for the Alcove in the King's Bedchamber at Greenwich (Fig. 147) in 1666 is Serlian. It was Webb's great achievement to coalesce all this into the majesty of the state rooms at Wilton.

The neo-Palladians start off with the disadvantage that there existed no corpus of interiors by either Jones or Webb. Campbell's dilemma is epitomised by the Wanstead House, Essex, section (Fig. 145) where the decoration of the hall is frankly in William Talman's Williamite taste with giant pilasters, bolection panelling and large inset paintings in the style of Ricci or Pellegrini. It is surely significant that this old-fashioned taste is evident in Campbell's Ebberston Lodge as late as 1718. However, with the decoration of Burlington House, about 1720, and the proposals for Mereworth Castle, Kent (Fig. 146) about 1722, Campbell has obviously been collecting ideas from The Queen's House, the Banqueting House, the St James's Chapel and Wilton – and perhaps, although it was never published, the interiors of St Paul's church, Covent Garden. The elements selected out of all this are often architectural in character: frames, *aedicules*, compartments, doors, and this is the moment in English neo-Palladian decoration when the elements of exterior architecture are brought indoors. Houghton Hall, Norfolk (Fig. 147) is a case in point. But once again, Chiswick is a watershed, and it was all due to John Talman's sale of the Jones–Webb drawings to Lord Burlington in 1720.

Here at first hand was a corpus of examples for the whole grammar of ornamentation and interior fitting, and with these, plus ancient Rome as represented by Desgodetz in 1684, Burlington and Kent worked out a canon of neo-Palladian decoration for Chiswick. When Kent published much of this in his *Designs of Inigo Jones* in 1727, all was available, not only to the architect with access to the books, but more important, to

Design attributed to Lord Pembroke for the Water House at Houghton Hall, Norfolk, *c.* 1730. *Courtesy Metropolitan Museum of Art, New York*

the pattern book compiler anxious to plunder or plagiarise. By 1728 Campbell had published his edition of Palladio's *First Book of Architecture*, which was re-issued by a bookseller in 1729 (the year after Campbell died) as *The Five Orders of Architecture* with several plates at the end of Campbell's interiors, and these were tremendously influential because country builders bought the edition, even if they already had Godfrey Richard's pocket edition of the *First Book* that had seen at least ten editions by 1733. The most influential book, however, was Isaac Ware's *Designs of Inigo Jones and others* that appeared as an undated edition not later than about 1733. Here was a rich Jonesian source, not only for interior decoration but for temples, alcoves, and gate piers, mostly by Jones and Webb, but some by Kent. Because it was a cheap book it secured a massive distribution with later editions in 1743 and 1756.

Kent's interiors can be wonderfully fanciful. He certainly had access to Jones's masque designs, but there was also the genius of his imagination that applied itself to furniture design, book illustration, gardens and painting. There is undoubtedly a spiritual link at least between Kent in the 1730s and Jones exactly a century earlier. It would be fascinating to know Lord Burlington's opinion of Kent's fancy, for the manner in which some of the Chiswick interiors are put together do not entirely accord with the authority of the exteriors. There is a hint here and elsewhere that Kent was mindful of such Venetian sixteenth-century interiors as those in the Doge's Palace, Venice. Kent's fancy, of course, can be seen as demeaning the purer classical treatment of the Burlingtonian interior, and well before Burlington's death in 1752 the architectural framework of interiors was becoming laced with rococo ornament, which itself can be seen as developing from baroque ornamentation, especially in plasterwork, that had been favoured by the likes of Gibbs or Leoni and executed by such as Artari and Bagutti. In printed form the rococo was introduced by Gaetano Brunetti in his *Sixty Different Sorts of Ornaments* in 1736. The weakening strength of neo-Palladianism is displayed by the work of second-generation Palladians, all devoted disciples of Burlington: by the 1750s Ware could execute full-blown French rococo interiors, and Vardy likewise (Fig. 156) mixed his architectural system with rich rococo pendants and cartouches. The Palladian dominance was certainly shorter-lived inside than outside, but then an interior was frequently a reflection of a patron's tastes or wishes, and an infusion of light rococo decoration was visually far more pleasing, especially to the ladies, than stricter and more sober architectural forms. The rococo influence coincides with changes in architectural draughtsmanship.

Burlington never presented a patron with a complete wall elevation; Kent in his painterly way did, but it was not until the age of the rococo that architects such as John Sanderson or Vardy made, as it were, a work of art out of an interior project. Designs were still made in two dimensions, but they were now intended to attract the patron, and the next step after the 1760s would be to feature a room in full three dimension, even to the placement of furniture. The introduction of colour is one of the more decorative aspects of designs by second-generation Palladians, and this in itself is symptomatic of the replacement of Burlington's austere and authoritative decorative programme by a more feminine and gayer one.

In summary, there has never been a period in English architecture since the national style of medieval gothic when a single style so dominated the whole country. It was strongest between 1715 and 1750, but neo-Palladian buildings would still be found as late as 1840, and Palladianism once again came into its own from the 1920s onwards. The Palladianism of Jones and Webb was a unique event, for nearly all the architecture of their subordinates in the court was closer in spirit to the manner of north European classicism, tinctured by the Jonesian court style. There were exceptions, of course, but it is noticeable that during the Protectorate the fashionable court style was then Artisan. Between Jones and Webb and Campbell and Burlington stand the styles of the second Stuart and Williamite courts: Anglo–Dutch, Anglo–French and Italianated Baroque, but generally a mix of everything. Neo-Palladianism was a reaction to this, and if Campbell initiated the architecture of reform, Lord Burlington gave it a stature that has mystified European historians ever since, because it was, in fact, neo-classical *avant la lettre*.

Illustrations

Dates are only given if drawings or designs are physically dated
Size: height before width in millimetres
Abbreviations: *c.* = circa
coll. = collection
Insc. = inscribed
All items illustrated are from the R.I.B.A. Collection unless otherwise stated.

INIGO JONES: NEWMARKET PALACE

Newmarket had always been a royal venue for the hunting. One of the earliest views, by Jan Siberechts in 1681, shows the small nucleus of the town dominated by the church and the King's House. This house was built for Charles II by William Samwell in 1668, and replaced Jones's Newmarket Palace. Very soon after his return from Italy, Jones was being employed for alterations and additions that reflect the sporting activities of the place. From 1615 to 1617 he built a dog-house, a stable, and brew house, in his capacity as Surveyor of the Works to James I. It was for Charles, Prince of Wales, however, that he built what may have been the most important building in his career, namely the Prince's Lodging. The year was 1619, the very same which saw his commission for the Banqueting House in Whitehall. The two are not unconnected in terms of facadism. Despite *Works's Accounts*, the actual planning of the Prince's Lodging is unknown. The two surviving elevations are certainly of a preliminary nature. They were meant to have served a street front, possibly on a corner, and we know that the side elevation possessed a straight cornice with an entablature which the attic window broke into. This entablature was not a normal one for it lacked a frieze, and it is this idiosyncracy that ties the astylar elevation to Newmarket (Fig. 2). In the other design, that is articulated with the orders of architecture, Jones has turned to his Palladio, his Scamozzi and his Serlio, but it should also be remembered that Lord Arundel possessed Scamozzi's original designs. The existence of this rich source poses a number of questions when seeking for the fount of Jones's inspiration. In this design (Fig. 1) there are no attic windows and the roof is lower, height being given to the ground floor pierced by tall windows with Serlian surrounds and keystone pressing up against the string course. It is the other design, the astylar one, that is so revolutionary. Height is now given to the roof with unusually tall attic windows, as if to provide views over the town to the exercising grounds. This is probably a brick house with stone coigns to the angles of the front and centre projection. If we draw a tree of development of the English country house, through the Caroline and Williamite periods, at its roots would stand this facade. There can be nothing more prophetic, and one of the first to recognize this was Sir Roger Townsend of Raynham Hall in Norfolk.

1 Inigo Jones. Elevation of an alternative front for the Prince's Lodging at Newmarket, Suffolk. Pen and wash (195 × 275)

2 Inigo Jones. Elevation of the 'accepted' astylar design for the Prince's Lodging at Newmarket, Suffolk. Pen and wash (195 × 280)

1

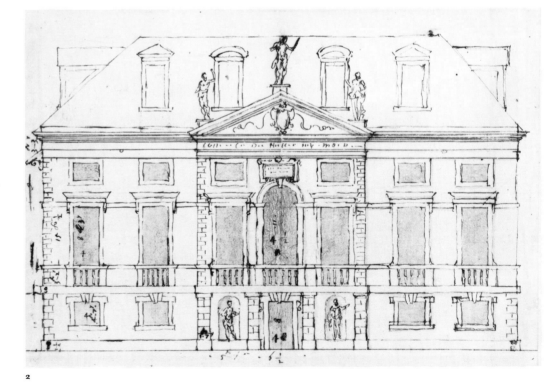
2

Inigo Jones had travelled to Copenhagen with the Duke of Rutland to present the Garter to King Christian in 1604. From 1605 onwards he was patronised by James Ist's Queen, Anne. In 1616 he was working for her at Oatlands Palace in Surrey and almost certainly nearby at Byfleet Palace where he may have added a classical portico to the Elizabethan house. Again in 1616 he was given a rather special task, to build a pavilion adjacent to the old ruined palace of Greenwich where the park was esteemed for the hunting and where Salomon de Caus had laid out a small mannerist grotto-garden. There is mystery surrounding the genesis of this new building, and ideas as to its use are only hypothetical. This plan (Fig. 4) is a rotunda with quadrant columnar arcades probably extending to pavilions, and derives from Scamozzi's Villa Pisani. The hall is 40 feet in diameter, the rooms in the corners 20 foot cubes, the portico 20 by 40, and the whole roughly 80 feet square. It is tempting to imagine this sited on the hill at Greenwich, like Palladio's famous Villa Capra or Rotonda.

As is well known, Jones decided upon a 'curious devise', to design an H-shaped building and to lay it across the public road that divided the park from the palace precincts, so that the stroke of the H formed a bridge. To this plan he provided various elevational solutions. This one (Fig. 3) is almost as astonishingly prophetic as the Newmarket design, for it is a villa, as understood by the neo-Palladians in the early 18th century. The determinant for such a design is that the fenestration of the front should be divided up into 1–3–1 bays, with the centre three slightly advanced and pedimented. Indeed, this actual design was copied for Lord Burlington, who thought it Palladio's. The portico is a *loggia*, and the inter-columnar balustrades are each separate, as at Scamozzi's Villa Molini, a fact noted by Jones in his copy of Palladio.

3 Inigo Jones. Elevation of a 'villa' facade, possibly for Greenwich. Pen and pencil (315 × 465)

4 Inigo Jones. Plan of a rotunda, possibly for Greenwich. Pen and wash (330 × 320)

3

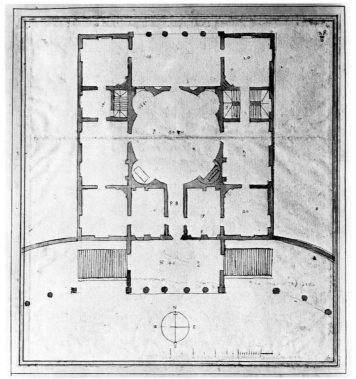

4

For ten years the Queen's House remained a shell. A painting of the south front shows the ground floor with a tall arched entrance flanked by four small arched windows, not at all what was built after 1630 represented here by this engraving from *Vitruvius Britannicus* (1715) (Fig. 6). In contrast to the south front which has been adequately recorded, this elevation may be the earliest record, and provides a truer picture than today when restoration has made the Queen's House look more neoclassic. Pairs of windows were clasped by iron balconies, and most astonishingly the areas of wall above the rusticated ground floor are indicated as painted with trophies and sacrifices (Fig. 5), just as on Italian mannerist facades. To sum up, it is difficult to believe that Jones in 1630 would have been content to execute a building designed right at the beginning of his career. Perhaps we should regard the Queen's House as a building of the 1630s – on the high plateau of Jones's development, rather than one at the beginning.

5 Unidentified draughtsman, perhaps English. Elevation of the north front of the Queen's House at Greenwich, showing proposed mural decorations

6 Engraving of south front of the Queen's House, Greenwich, from Colen Campbell, *Vitruvius Britannicus*, I (1715), pl. 15

5

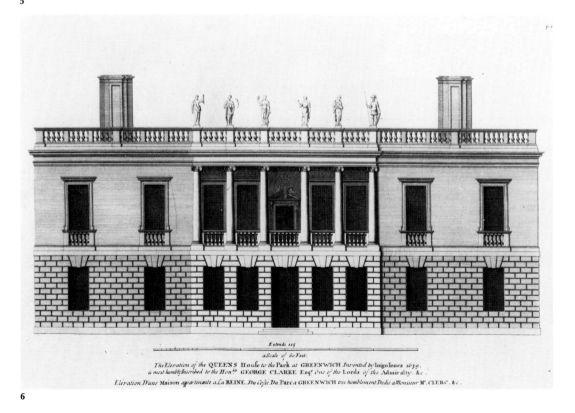

6

Raynham Hall is unquestionably one of the most remarkable houses to have survived from the age of Inigo Jones, for although not by Jones it is the most 'Jonesian' house of the period. It was certainly composed by its owner, Sir Roger Townsend, with the help of his mason and clerk of works, William Edge, but the possible 'approbation' of Jones (to use the word John Aubrey applied to Wilton) cannot be ignored. Although Townsend adopted a leisurely attitude to building his new house, slowly contemplating and changing it from about 1621 until the late 1630s, it draws upon much that Jones was designing before 1621, notably at Newmarket, which was on the road from Raynham to London. The centre-piece is clearly based upon Newmarket, as are types of Serlian windows, as drawn by Jones in 1618. The great pedimented gables with their scrolls were used by Jones on his design for Colonel Cecil's house in the Strand, London, before 1618. The plan of Raynham (Fig. 7), with its T-shaped saloon and hall, is taken from Palladio's Villa Pogliana. What is most noticeable about Raynham is the way the centre and the gabled ends project out from the body of the house. Basically the house is an E-shape and there is evidence that the tripartite windows on the first floor between the wings, if not the parts below, are an infill of the 1670s. If the first floor and upper part of Raynham were to be taken off and laid on the ground, there would be a remarkable resemblance to the Villa Maser with its temple centre and gabled wings. No other house at this time has quite the nobility of Raynham, which, despite the obviously empirical way in which Townsend and Edge put it together, succeeds in its classical convictions. To glimpse its stone-faced portico and the red brick of its elevations (Fig. 8) is to sense something of what has been lost at Newmarket.

7 'I.E.' (possibly I. Edge). Plan of ground floor, from album of survey drawings of Raynham Hall, Norfolk, prepared *c.* 1671. Pen and wash and pencil (420 × 540)

8 'I.E.' (possibly I. Edge). Elevation of the east front, from album of survey drawings of Raynham Hall, Norfolk, prepared *c.* 1671. Pen, wash and pencil (420 × 540)

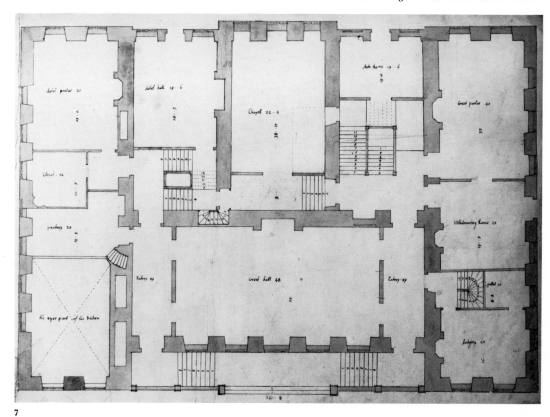

7

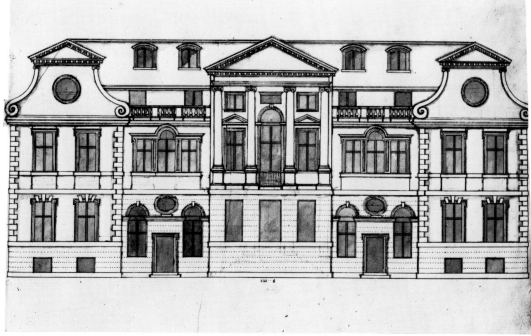

8

The garden gateway at 'East Bauly' dated 1623 is for the Marquis of Buckingham at Beaulieu or New Hall in Essex (Fig. 9). This particular gateway with its channelled masonry and three balls on the cornice provided an admired model for the neo-Palladians. Jones took particular delight in drawing and designing gateways, but then he was a master of the small scale unit of design, and he must have approached their creation with a certain inventive zeal. As with elements in his masque designs, he turned to engraved sources, for Hatton House (Fig. 14) and Oatlands (Fig. 13) to Serlio, for Arundel House (Fig. 11) to Vignola, or just occasionally as at New Hall to original drawings in his collection of Palladio's designs. The only gateway to survive is Lionel Cranfield, Earl of Middlesex's, modelled upon a Vignola gate at Villa Lanti. Burlington re-erected it at Chiswick in 1738, inscribing it with Pope's lines: 'Oh, Gate, how cam'st thou here?/I was brought from Chelsea last year,/Battered with wind and weather./Inigo Jones put me together,/Sir Hans Sloane Let me alone:/Burlington brought me hither'.

9 Inigo Jones, Gateway for New Hall, Essex, 1623. Pen and wash (350 × 305)

10 Inigo Jones. Gateway for Lionel Cranfield's house at Chelsea, London (later Beaufort House) 1621. Pen, pencil and wash (420 × 260)

11 Inigo Jones. Gateway, or more properly, doorway for Arundel House, Strand, London. Pen, pencil and wash (440 × 370)

12 Inigo Jones. Gateway for the Privy Garden, St James's Palace, London, 1627. Pen and wash (370 × 250)

9

10

11

12

13 Inigo Jones. Gateway for the Vineyard at
Oatlands Palace, Surrey. Pen, pencil and wash
(380 × 290)

14 Inigo Jones. Gateway for Hatton House,
Holborn, London. 1623. Pen, pencil and wash
(285 × 292)

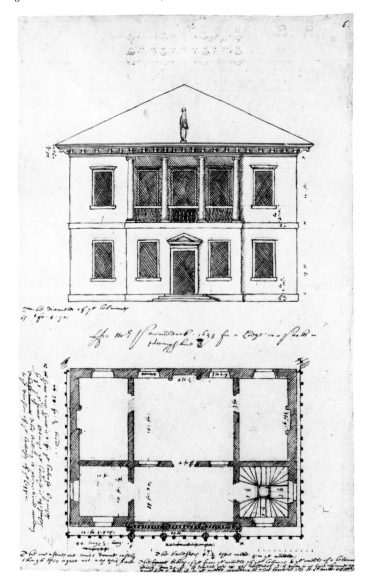

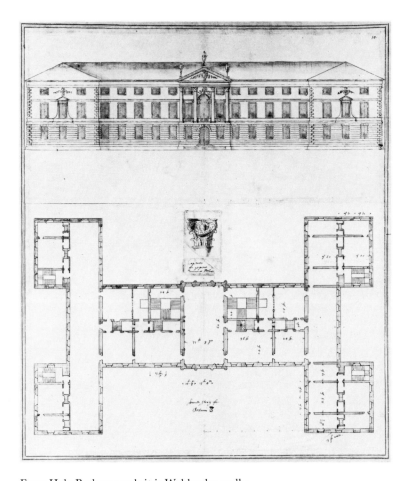

John Webb first comes into his own with Hale Park, Hampshire (Fig. 15), a *petite* and rustic version of the Queen's House. John Penruddock's 'Lodge in a Parke' was probably intended for hunting, although the date, 1638, soon after Penruddock inherited Hale, could mean a new house. Jones had built the church at Hale in 1631.

15 John Webb. A Lodge in Hale Park, Hampshire, 1638. Pen and pencil (350 × 220)

From Hale Park onwards it is Webb who really transmits the Jones court style into the vocabulary of the country house, hitherto the perquisite of Jones's subordinates. Unlike Jones, Webb seems to have been able to compromise with the Protectorate, probably through need. Belvoir Castle had been ruined by the Parliamentarians and in 1655 Webb saw the possibility of grandly rebuilding it. This was not to be, but there is evidence that Webb was responsible for a much simpler house using old walls and foundations. In this ideal project (Fig. 16) he is drawing upon Newmarket and his Scamozzi, and is beginning to express himself in more monumental language, clearly leading up to the King Charles II block at Greenwich of 1664.

16 John Webb. Plan and elevation for Belvoir Castle, Rutland and detail of capital for the Great Room. Pen and wash (445 × 380)

Although Webb's grand design for Belvoir (Fig. 16) was not built, it was engraved in *Vitruvius Britannicus*. This was also the case with Gunnersbury House in Middlesex (Fig. 17), save that Gunnersbury was built, and must have been regarded as an archetypal villa by the neo-Palladians. Webb built it for Sir John Maynard in 1658. The plan was based on a theoretical villa by Zanini but the elevations are made up of Jonesian parts: the *loggia* is a Corinthian version of the Queen's House; the proportions and line of each window bay come from the columnar Newmarket project. The Serlian windows with their voussoired heads are, however, closer to Raynham. On the ground floor there was a columnar under-hall, of a type that became more usual in neo-Palladian great houses with the *piano nobile* above.

The culmination of Webb's development is certainly Amesbury Abbey in Wiltshire built for the Duke of Somerset shortly before 1660. C.R. Cockerell in 1823 regarded it as of 'uncommon granduer'. Amesbury was not only engraved in Campbell's *Vitruvius Britannicus*, III, in 1725, but found an admiring place in Kent's *Designs of Inigo Jones* two years later. It was, of course, regarded as a design by Jones, despite the fact that Jones had died eight years earlier. The plan and silhouette proclaim a dependence upon Palladio's Villa Godi, but the proportions of the portico (Fig. 18) resembles Raynham, and beyond Raynham, the similar proportions of Newmarket. In general handling and surface decoration, however, and the heavily key-stoned windows, place Amesbury in the context of the Charles II block at Greenwich. Its most ingenious element was the staircase, a spiral within a square, derived either from Book 7 of Serlio or from the Palazzo Pallavicino as published by Rubens in his *Palazzi di Genova* in 1622. Amesbury was the model for Wilbury (Fig. 33) as well as providing ideas for Lord Burlington's Tottenham Park. Its state rooms may have been splendid, for a drawing reveals a simplified Wilton state room style.

17 John Webb *invenit*, Colen Campbell (or draughtsman) *delin*. Elevation of portico front of Gunnersbury House, Middlesex, drawn for plate 18 of *Vitruvius Britannicus*, I (1715). Pen (253 × 370)

18 John Webb *invenit*, Wyatt Papworth *delin*. Elevation of entrance front of Amesbury Abbey, Wiltshire, from a survey made in 1817 and copied by Papworth in 1840. Watercolour (710 × 1300)

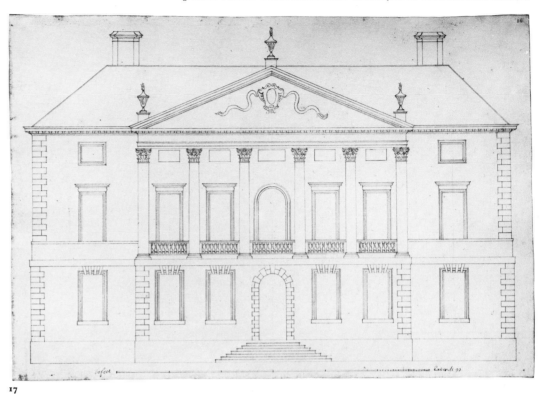

17

18

Webb's mandate at The Vyne, Hampshire, in 1654, was for the re-furbishing of an old Elizabethan house for Chaloner Chute. The garden front was re-fenestrated and the ends brought up as simple towers. In the centre Webb placed a noble portico partly *in antis*, the first free-standing portico to an English country house (Fig. 19).

This 18th century drawing (Fig. 20) is a proposal for adding towers to Butleigh Court, Somerset, the house built by Webb in the 1670s for his retirement and where all Jones's and Palladio's drawings were kept. No grand Palladian gestures here, but a house possessing the attractive idiosyncracy of Italianate tripartite *loggias* set *in antis* each end of the front, an idea taken up at Hatch Court, Somerset, in 1755.

19 Henry Flitcroft *delin.* Measured drawing of entrance front of The Vyne, Hampshire with wall plan and plan of Webb's portico. *Insc.* by Lord Burlington. Pen and wash (260 × 440)

20 Unidentified architect. Drawing of front of Butleigh Court, Somerset, with proposals for adding towers to Webb's house. Pen (235 × 380)

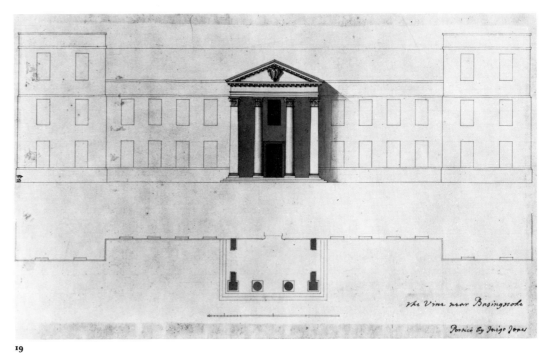

19

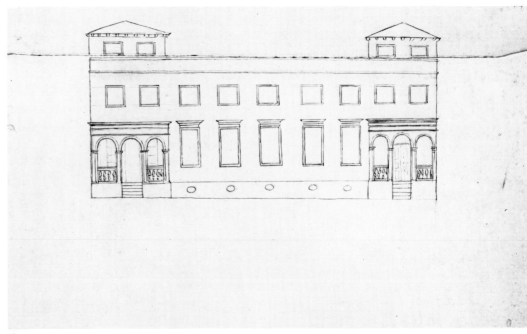

20

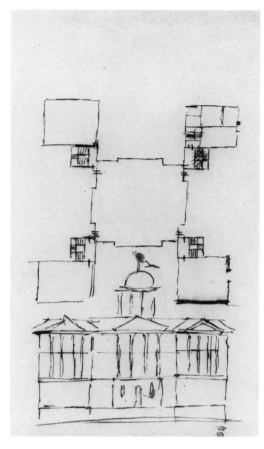

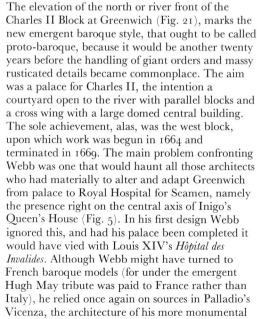

The elevation of the north or river front of the Charles II Block at Greenwich (Fig. 21), marks the new emergent baroque style, that ought to be called proto-baroque, because it would be another twenty years before the handling of giant orders and massy rusticated details became commonplace. The aim was a palace for Charles II, the intention a courtyard open to the river with parallel blocks and a cross wing with a large domed central building. The sole achievement, alas, was the west block, upon which work was begun in 1664 and terminated in 1669. The main problem confronting Webb was one that would haunt all those architects who had materially to alter and adapt Greenwich from palace to Royal Hospital for Seamen, namely the presence right on the central axis of Inigo's Queen's House (Fig. 5). In his first design Webb ignored this, and had his palace been completed it would have vied with Louis XIV's *Hôpital des Invalides*. Although Webb might have turned to French baroque models (for under the emergent Hugh May tribute was paid to France rather than Italy), he relied once again on sources in Palladio's Vicenza, the architecture of his more monumental town houses such as the Palazzi Valmarana or Thiene. What is more important is that Webb's canon of design at Greenwich provided the starting point for Wren, Vanbrugh and Hawksmoor in their completion of what was outwardly the most baroque ensemble of buildings in England.

As the devoted pupil of Jones, Webb could behave nonchalantly with some of his works. In 1663 the foundations were laid for adding four big, porticoed pavilions to the corners of the Queen's House (Fig. 22). Work was abandoned in 1669, but before this an architect, probably Webb, had filled in the spaces of the H so as to convert it into a square block.

21 John Webb. Design for north river front of Charles II Block at Greenwich. Pen (500 × 700)

22 John Webb. Rough perspective and plan for enlargement of Queen's House at Greenwich. Pen (200 × 325)

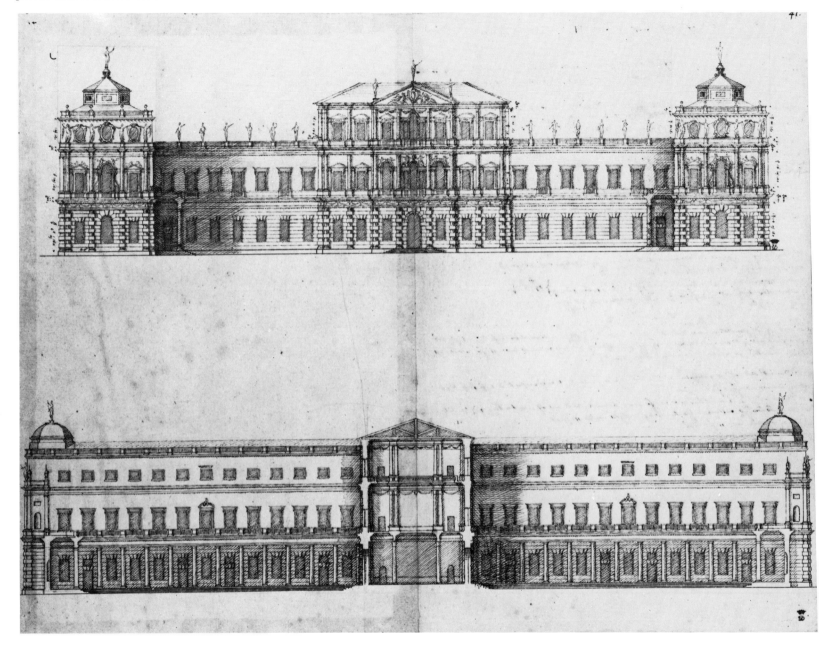

23 John Webb. Section, showing elevation of one
side of courtyard of a theoretical palace or public
building. Pen (330 × 440)

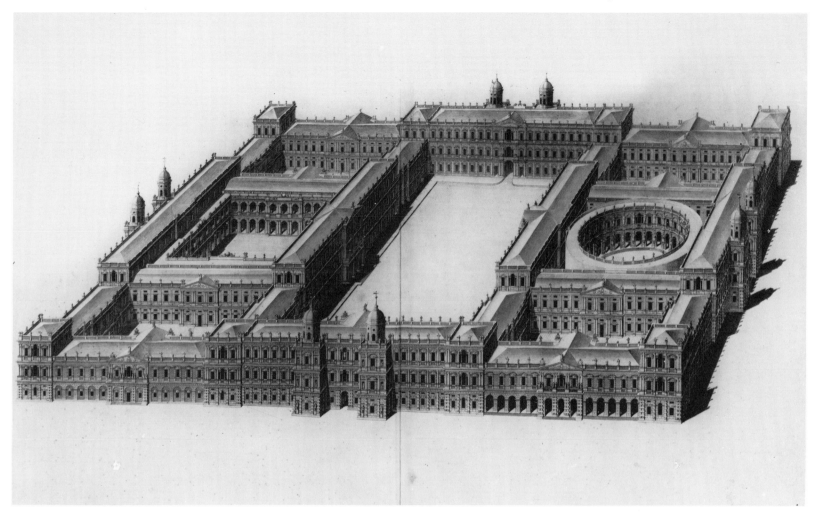

The whole problem of Jones's responsibility for a Whitehall Palace has been exacerbated by the fact, pointed out by J. A. Gotch as early as 1928, that not one drawing in his hand survives. Out of seven schemes, only one (called P) has been associated stylistically with Jones, for all of them are in Webb's hand (Fig. 23). The puzzling aspect of this situation is that even the P scheme (see p. 14) contains elements that do not appear in Jones's vocabulary before the 1630s, to which decade this scheme has been dated. It may well be that none of the schemes has anything to do with Jones. One point, however, ought to be made: as early as 1619 Rubens referred to Jones's Banqueting House not as a Banqueting House but as a palace, and although Jones was asked to build a Banqueting House he was obviously thinking of a *Sala Grande* in some hypothetical palace of the future in which the

Banqueting House would have served as one element. What, however, is far more important than deciding whether any scheme drawn by Webb was copied from a lost one by Jones, is that one scheme (the K scheme) (Fig. 24) was published by William Kent in *Designs of Inigo Jones and Others* in 1727, thus releasing to the neo-Palladian age a whole mass of material from which to quarry and borrow. The influence of Kent's engravings upon the general vocabulary of the age was profound, for it not only enabled architects to use Jonesian details with the stamp of authority, but the pattern book compilers such as William Halfpenny (Figs 103–4), Batty Langley, or William Salmon, plundered the Whitehall scheme for elements such as windows or doors to publish. The pattern book boom in England from about 1725 was the major force in spreading the new Palladianism throughout the

provinces. In towns such as Bath with sophisticated architects like John Wood the elder (Figs 107–8) or such as Stamford with minor figures like George Portwood, Webb's Palladian windows or rusticated and voussoired doorways can be found.

24 John Webb. Engraved perspective of a new palace sited in St James's Park, known as Kent's K scheme

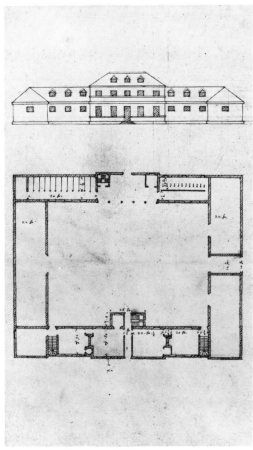

25

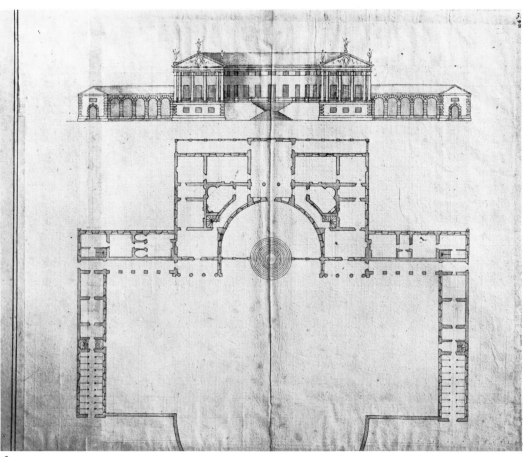

26

Webb's theoretical drawings (Figs 25–6) reflect the response of an architect trained by Jones to a variety of problems, mostly concerned with building types, the orders of architecture and parts of buildings. Many of the drawings must have been made after Jones's death in 1652, when Webb had leisure, but most must date back even earlier than the 1640s. It is unlikely that any belong to the very first years of Webb's apprenticeship, from the late 1620s. The method of presenting the drawings in terms of plan, elevation and sometimes sections, laid out neatly as if for publication as an engraved sheet suggests that a treatise was at the back of Webb's mind. This would be quite consistent with what we know of his academic approach to design rather than with the attitude of someone like Jones who saw himself as a connoisseur–artist–architect. Webb draws upon a variety of standard printed sources: Palladio, Serlio, Zanini, Philibert De l'Orme, Rubens's *Palazzi di Genova*, and especially Scamozzi. Not only are these authors held under tribute, but Webb drew also upon original drawings by Jones,

Palladio and others. He may also have been making copies after lost drawings by Scamozzi then in the Earl of Arundel's collection. His annotated Palladio and Serlio demonstrate that his reading was preparing the ground for a treatise and it is surely significant that a date, 1643, in his Serlio is the very year he was dismissed from the Office of Works. That dismissal gave him the time to prepare a treatise perhaps in anticipation of the ending of the Protectorate and his hopes of becoming the new Surveyor of the King's Works to Charles II. Alas, it was not to be.

25 John Webb. Plan and elevation for a farmhouse with stables and outbuildings situated around a courtyard. Although Webb's designs were not published, this one was selected by William Kent for his book in 1727. It thus became common property of the neo-Palladians, who were greatly concerned with designs for utilitarian buildings. Pen (355 × 232)

26 John Webb. Plan and elevation for a country house with a semi-circular concave front, its wings terminated by porticoes, a rendition of a house in the sixth book of Serlio, which plate in Webb's Serlio is profusely annotated as being a suitable design for a house situated on a hill (340 × 410)

27

Jones's friend was the 3rd Earl of Pembroke, not the 4th Earl who employed Isaac de Caus to rebuild Wilton. This (Fig. 27) is the design for a new facade on the old foundations to the old Tudor front; the Palladian towers by Webb (Fig. 28) are yet to come. Even so, de Caus has provided a bay element that was much copied by the later Palladians.

The myth of Wilton and Inigo Jones was first started by John Aubrey who claims that Jones gave his advice in the rebuilding programme after the fire of about 1648, for the 4th, and subsequently the 5th Earls of Pembroke. Webb is more likely to have converted de Caus's shell into a tower house thus providing a much copied prototype. Webb's suite of state rooms in the south front (Fig. 29) (Double Cube, Single Cube etc.) provide the sole remaining evidence of what royal rooms in the high Court style must have looked like. Even if not by Jones, these are what he would have designed.

27 Isaac de Caus. Elevation of the south front of Wilton, Wiltshire. Pen and pencil (155 × 440)

28 John Webb *invenit*. Colen Campbell *delin*. Elevation of the south front of Wilton, Wiltshire, drawn for plates 61–62 of *Vitruvius Britannicus*, II (1717). Pen and wash (209 × 500)

29 Plan of south front of Wilton as engraved for *Vitruvius Britannicus*, II (1717), plates 61–62

28

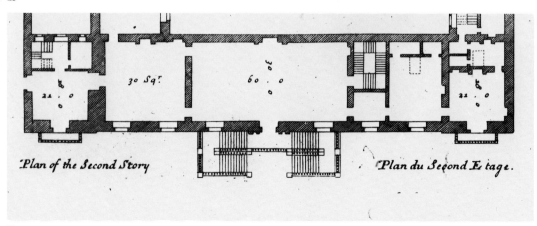

29

James Smith may prove to be an important figure in the story of neo-Palladianism, especially if he turns out to have been the catalyst in Colen Campbell's transition from lawyer to architect. Campbell regarded him as 'the most experienc'd Architect' of Scotland, and if he is the same Smith who was at the Scots College in Rome from 1671–75, it is likely that his interest in the architecture of Palladio goes back to this time. Smith was a Palladian *manqué*, because despite his theoretical fascination in Palladian plans and elevations, this interest did not extend to his executed work. This drawing (Fig. 30) is of Webb's New Gallery at Somerset House, London, built for the Queen Mother, Henrietta Maria, in 1662. It was based upon a Bolognese palazzo but proved of immense influence in London as a model for the Palladian town house. Campbell almost certainly copied this drawing for his engraving in *Vitruvius Britannicus* 1715, as the side bays were, in fact, never built.

30 James Smith. Project based upon John Webb's New Gallery. Pen and wash (290 × 470)

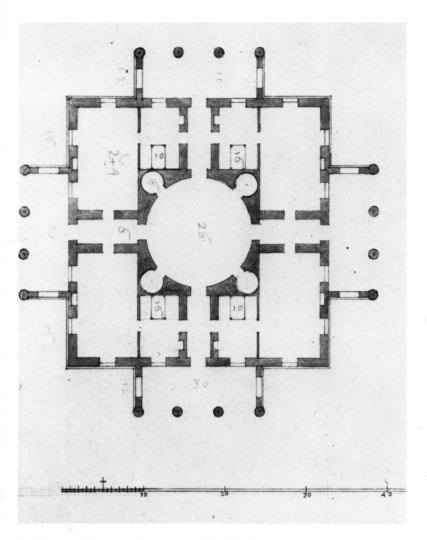

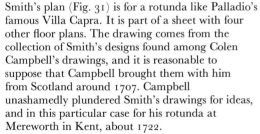

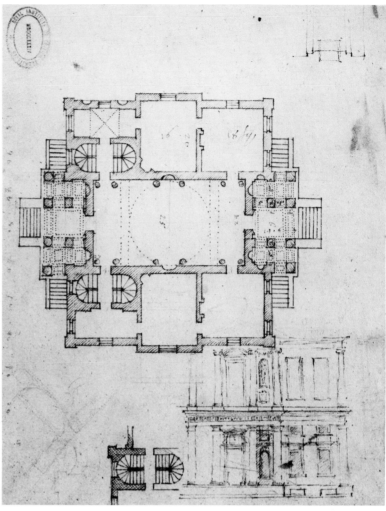

Smith's plan (Fig. 31) is for a rotunda like Palladio's famous Villa Capra. It is part of a sheet with four other floor plans. The drawing comes from the collection of Smith's designs found among Colen Campbell's drawings, and it is reasonable to suppose that Campbell brought them with him from Scotland around 1707. Campbell unashamedly plundered Smith's drawings for ideas, and in this particular case for his rotunda at Mereworth in Kent, about 1722.

31 James Smith. Plan of a rotunda villa. Pen and wash (490 × 372)

This drawing (Fig. 32) is by William or John Talman, but it does not really matter which, for the point is that this father and son partnership contributed to one of the largest collections of architectural drawings amassed around 1700. In that collection were the drawings by Palladio and Jones and Webb. In William's work Palladianism is incipient, for he is a baroque architect. Both he and John, however, were engaged in many projects for a Trianon at Hampton Court, and some studies, like this one, are Palladian in derivation.

32 William or John Talman. Plan and part elevation for a Palladian-inspired villa. Pen (195 × 274)

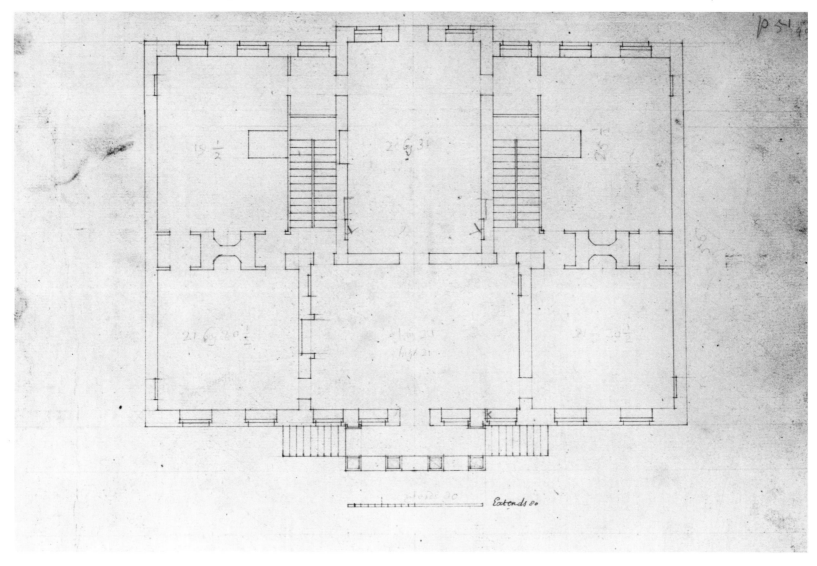

Wilbury House, Wiltshire, is the most important house in the opening phase of neo-Palladianism. Its plan (Fig. 33) is adapted from Palladio's Villas Sarego and Pogliana, but its facade (Fig. 34) is the top story of Amesbury laid down upon a low rusticated basement. The reason for this flagrant pinch from Amesbury concerns Wilbury's owner, William Benson, who played a significant role in the story of Campbell's rise to fame. In 1707 Benson married and in 1708 obtained a lease of Amesbury. Less than a year later he bought the adjoining manor of Newton Toney and there 'invented and built' to quote Campbell in *Vitruvius Britannicus*, 1715, a new Palladian villa. He named it Wilbury, supposedly made up of the *Wil* from Wilton and the

bury from Amesbury, both houses then, of course, acclaimed as works by Jones. Benson was obviously an amateur architect, perhaps not quite of the scholarly attainment of someone like Henry Aldrich, who at the time of his death in 1710 was compiling an *Elementa Architecturae* quoting from Vitruvius and Palladio as his chief authorities. Benson could be compared to a George Clarke, though there is no suggestion that Benson belonged to Clarke's Oxford coterie. Clarke's importance is that he owned about one half of the designs by Jones and Webb that had escaped from the main Webb collection, and these greatly influenced his many theoretical designs, some of which are astonishingly precocious for the years around 1710.

Both Clarke and Aldrich are shadowy figures: assessing their influence upon the advent of metropolitan Palladianism is difficult, but Benson is far more positive and to the fore. He must have played a major part in finding patrons for Campbell, perhaps even Sir Richard Child, for Wanstead in 1713. A few years later when Campbell was established, Benson's patronage becomes more public and obvious, for in 1718 he had ousted Sir Christopher Wren from the Surveyorship of the Works and this led to both he and Campbell plotting to replace the House of Lords with a new Palladian building. Obviously, Benson was something of an *eminence grise* to Campbell.

34

33 William Benson *invenit*. Colen Campbell *delin*.
Plan of Wilbury House, Wiltshire, *c.* 1708, drawn
for *Vituvius Britannicus*, I (1715), plate 51. Pen and
pencil (255 × 380)

34 William Benson *invenit*. Colen Campbell *delin*.
Elevation of Wilbury House, Wiltshire, drawn for
Vitruvius Britannicus, I (1715), plate 52. Pen and
pencil (255 × 380)

After 1706 Sir Richard Child at Wanstead in Essex had had George London lay out vast French formal gardens. The house was ancient and an owner of Child's enormous wealth must have contemplated a new one. His architect for the gardens was almost certainly William Talman. In consulting Colen Campbell, Child was turning from the chief architect of the old Williamite Court to the proponent of the new style. There is no evidence that any other architect vied for this great commission, and Campbell's coup was as astonishing as Vanbrugh's at Castle Howard. Indeed, it was Vanbrugh who ousted Talman there with a house in the then new baroque style. Campbell's first design for Wanstead is dated 1713, so before this he had only Shawfield near Glasgow to his credit, but this had been a direct pinch from one of Smith's designs.

Campbell published three designs for Wanstead House, Essex: in 1715 Wanstead I (Fig. 35), a slab-like, immobile block of 17 bays, and Wanstead II (Fig. 36) with the block contracted to 9 bays but the whole extended from 200 to 260 feet by the addition of lower wings comprising a *piano nobile* over a rusticated ground floor. This was executed, but without the dominating cupola. Then in 1720 he drew a theoretical project, Wanstead III (see p. 17) published in *Vitruvius Britannicus* (1725), for adding towers, each pierced by a Venetian window, precisely of the sort proposed for Houghton in 1723. The sources for Wanstead are Peckwater Quad out of an engraved design from Scamozzi's book. The bay disposition of the main block could come from Gunnerbury, as might the hall and saloon on the main axis. The stair cases, however, are set in the spine in the manner of Talman. Although both Wanstead I and II have the silhouette of Castle Howard, there is nothing in English architecture quite like the unadorned block of Wanstead I. Something of its purity of elevation can be found in the Whitehall Palace engraved by Campbell in *Vitruvius Britannicus* II (1717). Innovative also is the great hexastyle portico, seen as a true temple with its ridge passing right through the house to appear on the other side as a pilastered portico. The real influence of Wanstead was as a design on paper: *Vitruvius Britannicus* ensured that it served as the model, not only for the great house, but in reduced form for the Palladian villa with wings.

35 Colen Campbell. Elevation of Wanstead House, Essex, known as Wanstead I. Drawn for *Vitruvius Britannicus*, I (1715), plate 23. Pen and pencil (255 × 385)

The West Front of Wansted in Essex The Seat of Sr Richard Child Bar.^t

36

36 Colen Campbell. Elevation of Wanstead House, Essex, known as Wanstead II. Drawn for *Vitruvius Britannicus*, I, plates 24–25. Pen and pencil (265–660)

37 Colen Campbell. Plan of Wanstead I, drawn for *Vitruvius Britannicus*, I (1715), plate 22. Pen and pencil (255 × 380).

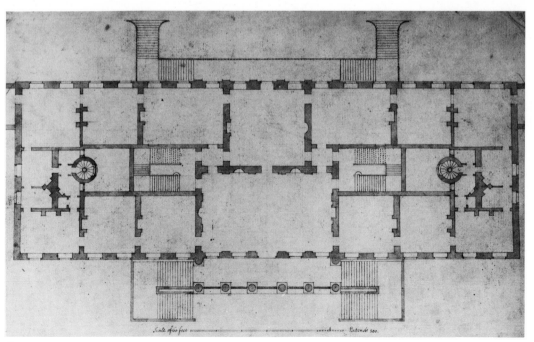

37

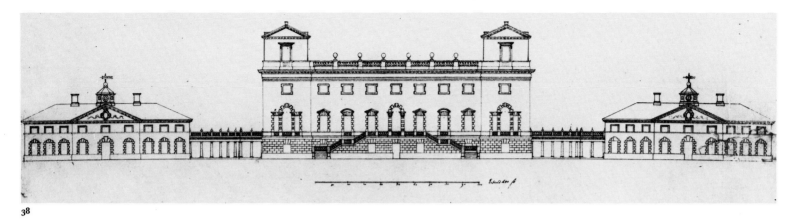

38

39

Campbell's career is marked by beacons each of which represent the successful promulgation of a Palladian building type. The villa is represented by Stourhead, the rotunda by Mereworth, the great house by Wanstead and the London terrace house by Grosvenor Square. Houghton (Fig. 38) is the most conspicuous adaptation of the tower house.

Houghton was begun for Sir Robert Walpole in 1722, by which time Campbell was the acknowledged master of Palladian synthesis. In fact he deals with a limited vocabulary of elements, used again and again, in this case (Fig. 39) from the garden fronts of Wanstead and Stourhead. More than anything, however, Houghton set the seal on the fashion for the pavilion or tower house.

38 Colen Campbell. Elevation of the east front of Houghton Hall, Norfolk, as engraved for *Vitruvius Britannicus*, III (1725), plates 29–30. Pen (210 × 510)

39 Colen Campbell. Elevation of west front of Houghton Hall, Norfolk. Pen and wash (305 × 455)

Stourhead in Wiltshire was built for Henry Hoare from 1720, and William Benson, a relation, seems to have been consulted. Stourhead lies with Newby as the first of Campbell's expositions of the villa theme. Basically Campbell took Palladio's Villa Emo at Fanzolo both in plan and elevation, modifying the plan somewhat and drawing the protico *in antis* out as a full portico. There is far more individuality on the side elevations with their variety of heavily rusticated and blocked windows and bold central Palladian doorway. Like Sir John Soane later, Campbell had great facility in paraphrasing motifs and elements, so versions of this Stourhead facade appear at Houghton in 1722, and in 1724 at Plumptre House, Nottingham and on the unexecuted designs for Goodwood. He first uses sequences of these windows at Wanstead in 1713–15.

40 Colen Campbell. Elevation of the east front of Stourhead, Wiltshire, as engraved for *Vitruvius Britannicus*, III (1725), plate 42. Pen and wash (332 × 499)

41 Colen Campbell. Elevation of the east front of Stourhead, Wiltshire, as engraved for *Vitruvius Britannicus*, III (1725), plate 43. Pen and wash (324 × 480)

40

41

Although the inspiration to first design a version of Palladio's Villa Rotonda (Fig. 43) or Capra at Vicenza must be James Smith's, it is to Campbell's credit (Fig. 42) that he actually built one, for John Fane at Mereworth in Kent in 1722. It is the closest in imitation to Palladio's original, but larger, being a square of 90 feet compared to 80, and no other neo-Palladian rotunda in England is so convincingly Palladian. Campbell spawned four others, all departing from the original in certain respects. There was Chiswick in 1725, Foots Cray about 1754, Nuthall Temple, 1754, and an unidentified one by John Sanderson. Although Campbell's achievement at Mereworth was somewhat imitative, he compensated for this by setting the villa in a moat and bridging it from two of the porticoes.

42 Colen Campbell. Plan of villa and moat and elevation of front with section through moat. Pen and wash (730 × 510)

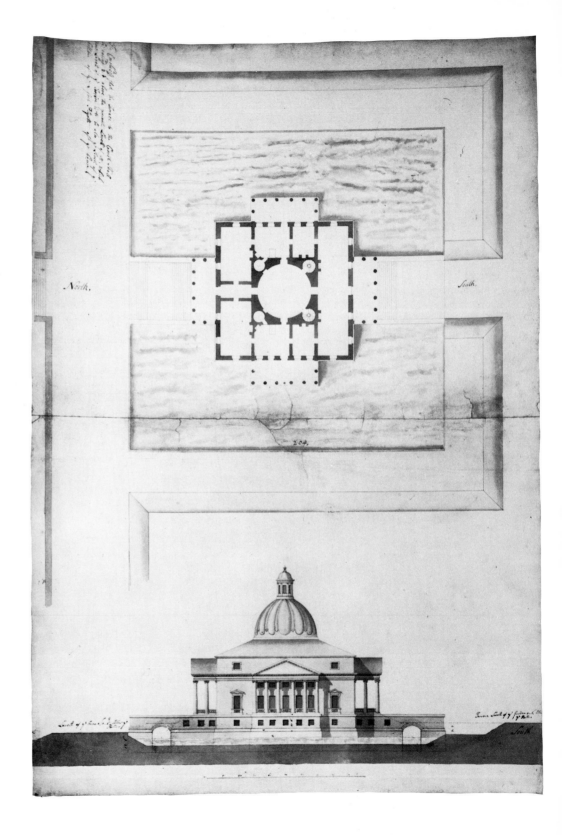

43 Andrea Palladio. Engraving of the Villa Rotonda or Capra, Vicenza, Italy

Campbell brought the villa to town in the guise of Pembroke House, Whitehall, built for Henry Herbert the 9th Earl of Pembroke, and finished in 1724. Its starting date is disputed for Herbert acquired the site in 1717. Country houses in England with first floor loggias are rare. There are also the Queen's House and Gunnersbury, although it is a mystery as to whether Jones's Lodge at Bagshot Park in Surrey, built in 1631, survived into the 18th century. At Pembroke House Campbell seems to have amalgamated a villa with a temple-like portico *in antis* carried on three rusticated arches or arcades. There is certainly an echo of Vanbrugh's Bagnio at Eastbury. There is also another innovation namely the horizontal division of the facade by string courses. Out of Pembroke House comes Marble Hill, Middlesex, designed by Lord Pembroke and Roger Morris in about 1724, and as this is so close in time to Pembroke House, his lordship's intervention in the design cannot be discounted. Indeed the first floor plan is so unlike Campbell's standard arrangement, that its columnar idiosyncracies should perhaps be attributed to Pembroke. By virtue of being in an urban situation, as well as having been engraved in *Vitruvius Britannicus* (Fig. 44), Pembroke House must have exercised an appreciable influence.

Campbell was astute enough to recognize the main chance in the boom in London estate development in the 1720s. On Lord Burlington's own estate behind Burlington House, it was Campbell who designed nos 31–34 Old Burlington Street. These four houses were fronted by a common astylar facade, joined only by a string course. There were precedents: in Jones's own Maltravers development in Lothbury in the City, and more notably as far as the proportioning of the upper floors is concerned, in the piazzas at Covent Garden. There were others. It was Campbell's cleverness to innovate a standard astylar street front out of these earlier essays. His hopes in 1725 to design a whole side of Grosvenor Square (Fig. 45) were not realised, but here again he took the basic framework of Covent Garden (with recollections of Peckwater Quad) and gave it a more genuine, Palladian air. The result set up echoes, firstly in Bath and then in other towns.

44 Colen Campbell. Plans and elevation of Pembroke House, Whitehall, London, as engraved for *Vitruvius Britannicus*, II (1725), plate 48. Pen (380 × 255)

45 Colen Campbell. Elevation for Grosvenor Square, London. Pen and wash (325 × 510)

44

45

COLEN CAMPBELL: THE TOWN HOUSE

Campbell may have come into Lord Burlington's orbit as early as 1717 because this is the year given by Campbell to the Bagnio at Chiswick when he engraved it in *Vitruvius Britannicus* III and described it as 'the first essay of his Lordship's happy invention'. It was a Campbellian composition, not unlike elements in the Campbell/Emmett Whitehall designs, and as a bay motif it was paraphrased by Campbell to fit the end bays of Burlington House in Piccadilly. For the rest Campbell turned to Palladio's Palazzo di Iseppo da Porto in Vicenza and a rusticated Jonesian basement. However derivative all this may have been, Campbell had scored with the first Anglo-Palladian town house in London (Fig. 46). It was not a model for emulation because of its special position and the fact that Campbell's challenge was to remodel an earlier house.

This 'Design for the Hon: Henry Pelham Esqr. begun 1720 in Burlington Gardens but never finished C:C:' (Fig. 47) belongs to the period when Lord Burlington was developing his estate behind Burlington House and employing Campbell. It seems to have been on the site of numbers 31 to 34, subsequently built over by Campbell's famous group of four astylar houses. Why it was never completed is not known, but it is puzzling that number 30, Mountrath House, was a very close, but slightly more urbane, version by Lord Burlington of this design. The central first floor window became a popular Palladian element: it derives firstly from Jones's St James Chapel and also from the Whitehall designs published by Kent and known to Campbell.

46

46 Colen Campbell. Elevation of south front of Burlington House, Piccadilly, London. Pen and wash (255 × 310)

47 Colen Campbell. Elevation for Henry Pelham's house, Burlington Gardens, London. Pen and wash (520 × 345)

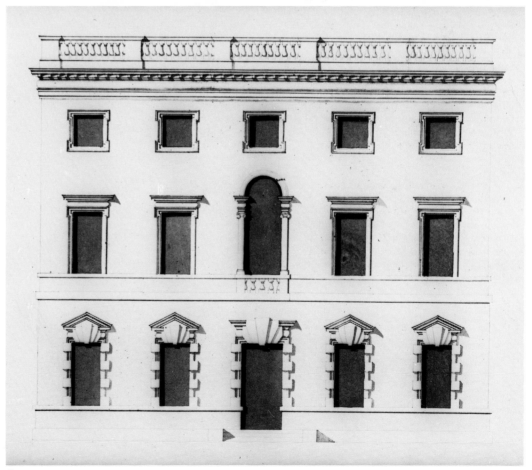

47

69

When *Vitruvius Britannicus* I was published in 1715 the up-and-coming country house architect was James Gibbs, who steers a very cleverly-contrived course between the baroque and Palladianism, never indulging in the extremes of either. Like Sir William Chambers later he was a middle-of-the-road eclectic. This design for rebuilding Lowther Castle, after a fire in 1717 (Fig. 48), shows how much Gibbs was beginning to conform to the new fashion. Although details like brackets to the windows belong to the baroque vocabulary of someone like William Talman, the facade and its portico betrays the restraint that was to grow in Gibbs's work.

The appearance of volume one of *Vitruvius Britannicus* in 1715 was undoubtedly a warning to Sir John Vanbrugh that his popularity as a baroque architect could begin to wane. Palladian elements appear in his work from about 1718 onwards, most notably at Eastbury in Dorset (1718) and Seaton Delaval in Northumberland (1720). At Grimsthorpe Castle in Lincolnshire he almost makes a *volte face*, for the north front of 1722, with a centre in Vanbrugh's best theatric style, was given terminal pavilions that would have pleased Lord Burlington almost more than those at his own London house. The most astonishing turn-about for Vanbrugh, however, occurred when he came to design the unexecuted south front of Grimsthorpe. This (Fig. 49) is a paraphrase of Campbell's Houghton then being built (but not engraved until 1725).

48 James Gibbs. Elevation of portico front proposed for Lowther Castle, Westmorland about 1725. Pen and wash (350 × 510)

49 Sir John Vanbrugh *invenit*. Colen Campbell *delin*. Elevation of unexecuted garden front of Grimsthorpe Castle, Lincolnshire, as engraved for *Vitruvius Britannicus*, III (1725) Pen (205 × 375)

48

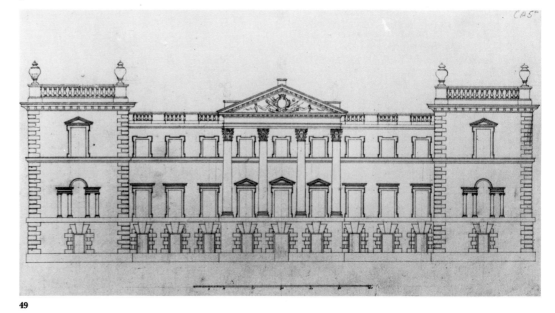

49

Lord Burlington's first opportunity to display his skills as an amateur architect occurred in 1720 when he was invited by his brother-in-law, Lord Bruce, to rebuild the family mansion at Tottenham Park in Wiltshire. This (Figs 50–52) was the first true neo-Palladian tower house, but, as yet, uninfluenced by the drawings of Jones and Palladio.

To create Tottenham, Burlington looked at a number of sources. The plan (Fig. 50) of his main block is a little like Palladio's Villa Pojana, but over the corner rooms Burlington raises four towers, the most obvious source for the garden front being the Villa Tornieri. In the middle of the house is a tower with cupola, *à la* Amesbury. The novelty of Tottenham is its primacy as a true Palladian tower house with Palladian windows set in the tower fronts: these are fractionally earlier than Houghton. The entrance front (Fig. 51) was also towered, but without the Palladian windows. The centre-piece was rather curious. Below the pediment were five closely-spaced windows, in front of which was set a low Ionic hexastyle portico with a straight balustrade. On a vaster scale Jones built this type of straight portico at old St Paul's Cathedral. The wings at Tottenham were not added until the late 1730s after the experiences at Chiswick.

50 Lord Burlington *invenit*. Another *delin*. Plan of Tottenham Park, Wiltshire, with wings as built *c.* 1737.

51 Lord Burlington *invenit*. Henry Flitcroft *delin*. Elevation of the entrance front of Tottenham Park, Wiltshire. Pen and wash (260 × 311)

52 Lord Burlington *invenit*. Henry Flitcroft *delin*. Elevation of garden front of Tottenham Park, Wiltshire, 1721. Pen and wash (215 × 225)

51

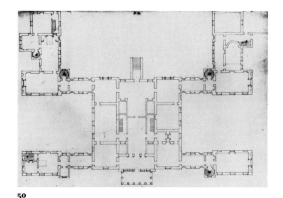

50

52

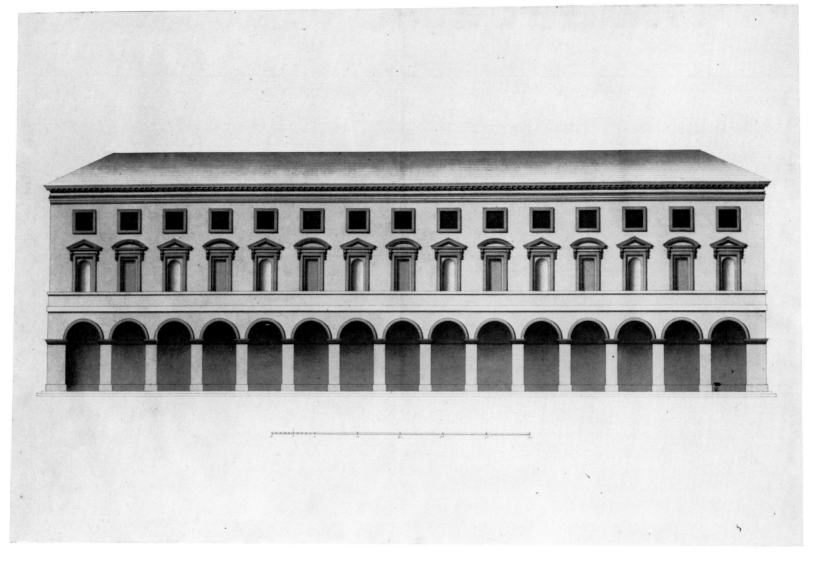

The Westminster Dormitory (Fig. 53), whose foundation stone was laid 21 April 1722, has been singled out as demonstrating the triumph of the new emergent style of neo-Palladianism against the baroque of Wren, Hawksmoor and William Dickinson. This is a fact, but it is really the triumph of one architect against another, of Lord Burlington against Dickinson. Dickinson had been producing designs since 1712 and as late as 1721 had tried to match Burlington's Palladian design with one of his own, but to no avail. The Dormitory was not Burlington's first essay in architecture, for it was preceded by Tottenham by about a year. It was, however, a public building, and undoubtedly rammed home the message that Jones and Palladio were in and Wren and Vanbrugh were out. The requirements for the Dormitory were a dormitory above and rooms below with some form of outside circulation. An arcade or cloister was obviously desirable, and Burlington recognized an appropriate model in one of the facades of Covent Garden by Inigo Jones. Stripped of its Tuscan order, here was the arcade, the main story, and a low story above lit by a square window. There is nothing like the Dormitory in Palladio, and although Burlington turned to Jones for a model, his details and treatment of the surfaces has imbued the building with an unusual severity and restraint, almost coldly neoclassical *avant la lettre*.

53 Lord Burlington *invenit*. Henry Flitcroft *delin*. Elevation of The Dormitory, Westminster School, London, as engraved for William Kent, *Designs of Inigo Jones . . . With Some Additional Designs*, 1727, vol. 2, plate 51. Pen and wash (345 × 525)

54

55

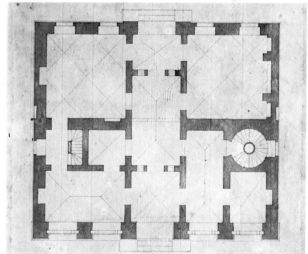

56

In creating for General George Wade in 1723 at 29 Old Burlington Street, a small palazzo based upon a design by Palladio, Burlington was not being a plagiarist. In 1751 Count Algarotti could acknowledge this derivation as a fact without criticism, for he, like Burlington, understood the theory of imitation which approved the copying from an old master. It was certainly one of the handsomest fronts in London, where, in Ralph's words, the 'decorations were perfectly proportion'd to the space they were to fill'. The front (Fig. 54) was, in fact, a back elevation facing a courtyard, somewhat in the French manner. As Wade was a highly cultured patron and close friend of

Burlington's, it is likely that there was close consultation in the design, and Wade may even have selected the model from the Palladio collection. It is the first instance of Burlington turning to his Palladio drawings (Fig. 55) for use and inspiration. When Sir John Clerk visited Burlington in 1727 he specifically noticed the appropriateness of the Doric order, 'intended for a military man . . . because antiently . . . monuments . . . to Heroes were of this order'. The plan (Fig. 56) was modified in execution as shown by *Vitruvius Britannicus* III, 1725. Apart from Burlington House, no other front on London possessed such an impeccable Vicentine ancestry.

54 Lord Burlington *invenit*. Henry Flitcroft *delin*. Elevation of court front of 29 Old Burlington Street, London. Pen and wash (360 × 265)

55 Andrea Palladio. Elevation for a town house. Pen and wash

56 Lord Burlington *invenit*. Henry Flitcroft *delin*. Plan of ground floor of 29 Old Burlington Street, London. Pen and wash (360 × 270)

57 Lord Burlington *invenit*. Henry Flitcroft *delin*. Elevation of the south front of Chiswick House, London, as engraved but to smaller scale for

William Kent, *The Designs of Inigo Jones . . .*, 1727, Pen and wash (310 × 370)

The history of Chiswick is one of additions to the old Jacobean house. By 1716 gardens were being remodelled with *allées* terminated by temples, one, the Casina, by Burlington in 1717, another in the style of James Gibbs. Between 1720 and 1725 Burlington was laying out part of the gardens with basons of water and temples. The new villa was begun about 1726 with no link to the old house, but already the entrance front of this house had been remodelled (Fig. 58) a three bay design that only faintly acknowledges Palladio or antiquity. When Burlington began, he had thoroughly digested Palladio's drawings, and plans and parts of elevations are based upon Palladio's models. Chiswick is the most strictly disciplined of all Palladian houses, perhaps even more than Palladio's own, and the way in which almost every single detail can be found in Palladio, Palladio's drawings of Roman antiquity, or Roman antiquity as recorded by Desgodetz, makes it academically of the utmost fascination, but also, it must be admitted, renders it somewhat pedantic. It was smaller than its Vicentine prototype, and as a rotunda less obviously Palladian in derivation than Campbell's Mereworth. In fact, Burlington was as much influenced by Scamozzi's Villas Rocca Pisani and Molini as by the Villa Rotonda. Chiswick was engraved by Kent in 1727 and extolled as the villa *par excellence*. Its elevational composition (Fig. 57), particularly the garden front with a sequence of three Venetian windows, and its plan (Fig. 59) with shaped, Roman-derivative rooms, resounded throughout British architecture for over three centuries.

58 Lord Burlington *invenit*. Another *delin*. Floor plans and elevation for adding new frontispiece to the old house at Chiswick. Pen, pencil and wash (350 × 470)

59 Lord Burlington invenit. Ground floor plan of Chiswick House, London, as drawn by John White in 1788 for the addition of wings to the villa. Pen and wash (195 × 265)

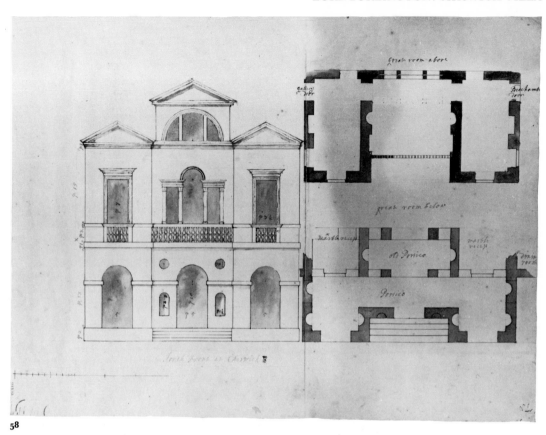

58

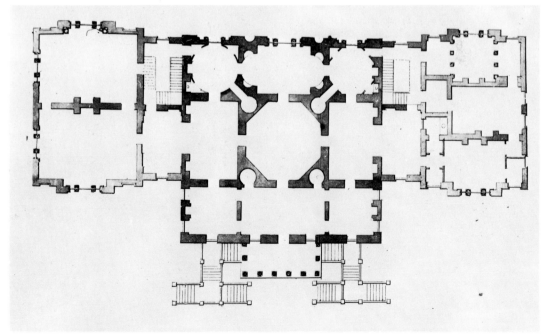

59

LORD BURLINGTON: CHISWICK VILLA

In placing his new villa a short distance to the north west of his old house, Burlington at once created a problem that would have to be solved in due course, namely how to link the old with the new. There is no evidence that he intended to demolish the old house, which was substantial and had, of course, been refronted. Rysbrack's set of paintings of Chiswick gardens made shortly before 1730 do not include any views of the new villa from the north or any parts of the gardens from north to east. This would suggest that these parts were only remodelled after 1730, and there is the added confirmation of this from Rigaud's views made in 1733 to 1734, which do show this area. Rigaud shows what became known as the Link Building, a link or corridor connecting the north-east angle of the villa to an extension of the north end of the old house, thus creating a three sided court, on the west the east side of the villa, on the north the south front of the Link Building, and on the east a tripartite columned loggia above an arcade. The creation of this *petite* courtyard by means of the Link is probably one of the 'beautiful additions' referred to by Sir Thomas Robinson in December 1733, and over which Horace Walpole effused: 'the classic scenery of the small court that unites the old and the new house, are more worth seeing than many fragments of ancient grandeur, which our travellers visit under all the dangers attendant on long voyages'. When the Link Building was externally completed about 1735 the view from the north embraced what can only be described as a staccato sequence of parts, each of a unity, but joined by walls slightly recessed. This concatenation was to exert great influence: on the wings at Holkham from about 1734 and at Tottenham Park from about 1736 when Burlington added wings to that house. This staccato, additative, method of designing was the basis of William Kent's style.

60 Lord Burlington *invenit*. Henry Flitcroft *delin*. Plan and elevation of south front for the addition of a Link Building to Chiswick House, London. Pen and wash (340 × 310)

61 Detail from engraved view by J. Roque, 1736, showing the Chiswick villa, the Link Building, and the Summer Parlour

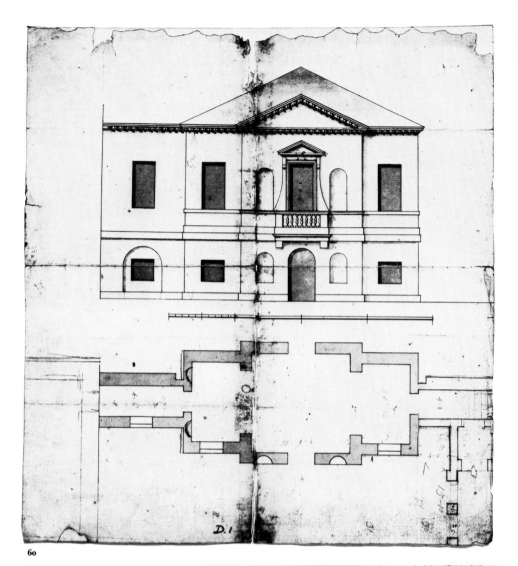

60

61

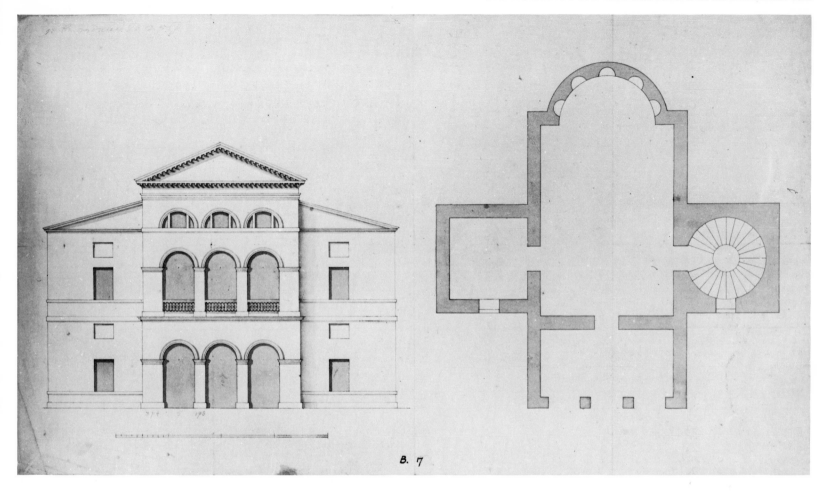

B. 7

The Westminster Dormitory and the York Assembly Rooms stand at the two polarities of Burlington's career, the one drawing basically upon Inigo Jones, the other upon Palladio and Roman antiquity. The Chichester Council House project (Fig. 62, Plate X p. 34) for the 2nd Duke of Richmond, who lived nearby at Goodwood, is dated 1730, a year before York. Burlington took for model an exchange with open arcades on the ground and an arcaded ambulatory above surrounding the hall, lit by Diocletian windows. Palladio's Basilica at Vicenza is, of course, its starting point. As a totally arcuated astylar design it has no obvious precedent and could have been built in Revolutionary Paris. A reduced design repeated the front elevation but set it within side bays and intersecting pediments, to a plan of an apsed temple type.

62 Lord Burlington *invenit*. Henry Flitcroft *delin*. Street elevation of reduced design for proposed Council House at Chichester, Sussex. Pen and wash (350 × 620)

Chiswick undoubtedly marks a point of departure
for Burlington, as witness to a style that is an
interpretation of ancient and modern architecture,
and this, for Burlington, culminated in his York
Assembly Rooms (Figs 63–5) conceivably the most
novel and significant building in Europe at the
time. Designs were requested in May 1730 and the
foundation stone laid in March 1731. His problem
was to design a grand festival hall, so he would
obviously see how the ancients did this. Therefore
Burlington set himself the task of reviving a
Vitruvian structure as interpreted by Palladio. The
latter called his hall an Egyptian Hall, providing a
width of six columns. As Palladio remarked that the
'Egyptian Hall resembles Basilicas very much',
Burlington turned to Palladio's ancient basilica to
find a recommended length of eighteen columns.
The hall prefaced by an apsidal-shaped vestibule
had the authority of Vitruvius, as in the Barbaro
edition, drawn by Palladio and published in 1556.
For his novel facade Burlington started out with the
Roman Temple of Bacchus as published by
Palladio, but imaginatively framed the whole by
columnar screens based upon the Roman Baths, as
published by Burlington himself in the *Fabbriche
Antiche* of 1730. Out of the Assembly rooms comes
the hall at Holkham, which exercised a resounding
effect upon halls, assembly rooms, great halls, and
later the public areas of museums, hotels and
railway stations. For Burlington everything
culminated at York. There were certainly later
works, but after York nothing can really be added
to Burlington's achievement. York was unique.

63 Lord Burlington *invenit*. Henry Flitcroft *delin*.
Plan of the Assembly Rooms at York. Pen and wash
(300 × 450)

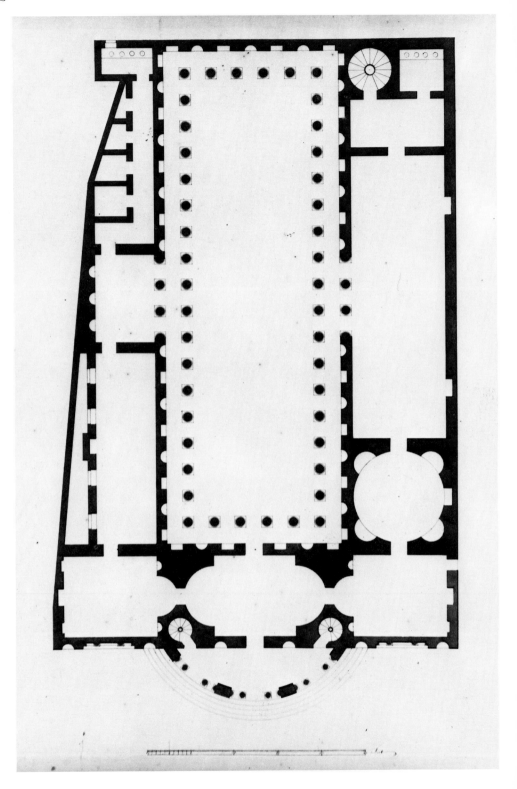

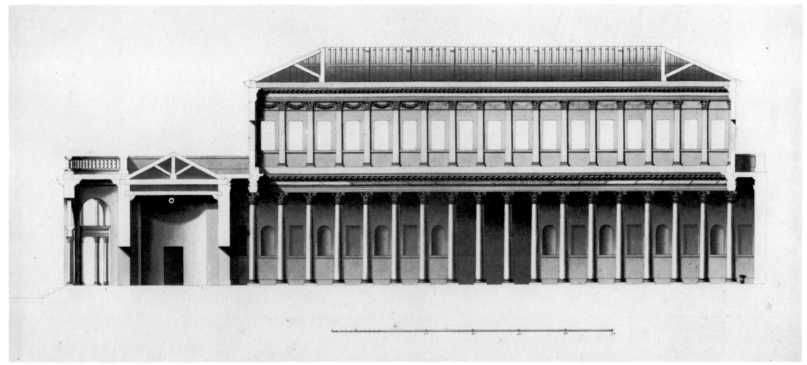

64

64 Lord Burlington *invenit*. Henry Flitcroft *delin*. Longitudinal section through the Assembly Rooms at York. Pen and wash (395 × 540)

65 Lord Burlington *invenit*. Henry Flitcroft *delin*. Elevation of the Assembly Rooms at York. Pen and wash (350 × 620)

65

At about the time that Lord Burlington was engaged upon producing designs for the Council House at Chichester for the 2nd Duke of Richmond, he was commissioned to design the Duke's new house in Whitehall, and, happily for Burlington, this was built. The documentation on Richmond House is so scanty that it is not known if these designs (Figs 66–9) were executed in detail. Canaletto shows a corner of the house in 1746 with a projecting bay on one front and the roof carrying obelisk chimney stacks as on Chiswick. Burlington's plan (Fig. 66) is an ingenious one incorporating a large circular staircase and a number of satisfactorily-shaped rooms that spill over into an extension on one front so providing large window recesses or vestibules. The designs for ceilings (Figs 68–9) give the only hint as to the character of the interior decoration, and these are firmly Jonesian, of the Queen's House type.

66 Lord Burlington *invenit*. Another *delin*. Plan of the 'Principal Storey' of Richmond House. Pen and wash (220 × 175)

67 Lord Burlington *invenit*. Another *delin*. Elevation for the front of Richmond House. Pen and wash (220 × 180)

68 Lord Burlington *invenit*. Another *delin*. Design for the drawing-room ceiling, Richmond House. Pen and wash (190 × 175)

69 Lord Burlington *invenit*. Another *delin*. Design for the ceiling of the 'Salon Room', Richmond House. Pen and wash (200 × 180)

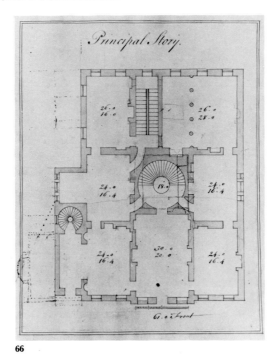

66

67

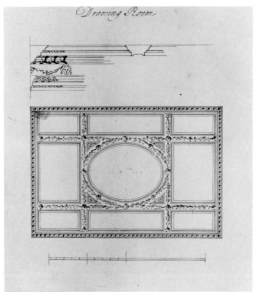

68

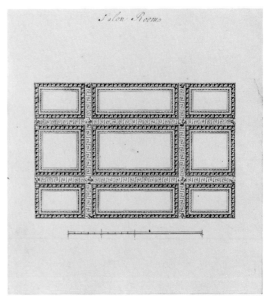

69

William Kent's character, jolly and extrovert, in contrast to Lord Burlington's coolness and asceticism, is expressed in his architecture which is outwardly staccato and full of movement. By 1732, when he was working upon the Royal Mews, he had already developed a style that owes much to the inspiration of the Chiswick Link Building. It is difficult to know just how much of Burlington is behind Kent, so close were they as persons, if not lovers. In 1732 Burlington had been asked to examine Hawksmoor's designs for a new Parliament House and in 1733 the *Gentleman's Magazine* could report 'The Earl of Burlington has projected a Plan for building two new Houses of Parliament, and a Public Library between them'. From 1733 until 1739 Kent was busy drawing up various schemes, presumably with Burlington's approval. There were many developments of plan and elevation, with many astonishing projects of a columnar nature based upon the Roman Baths. The final submission of December 1739 was more restrained, but was noteworthy for its great temple feature in the form of a towering dome 160 feet high. All the vocabulary of the neo-Palladians was employed here, with allusions to Chiswick, the Jonesian Whitehall designs, Holkham, and Kent's own Treasury Buildings of 1733. Something of the abortive Houses of Parliament survives in Kent's Horse Guards begun in 1749 but completed by John Vardy after Kent's death. Had this colossal and grandiose scheme been executed, Kent's name, if not Burlington's, would have been as well known as Wren's. There can be no doubt that both Kent and Burlington saw in their designs their neo-Palladian response to Inigo Jones's Palladian Whitehall Palace. Had the Houses of Parliament design been engraved, the life of neo-Palladianism might have been strengthened if not extended.

Gothick is not, of course, Palladian, but it was accepted that architects could be ambidextrous, and gothick (with a k), or rococo gothic as it is sometimes called, was practiced by many staunch Palladians, including Flitcroft, Ware, Kent, Garrett, but significantly not Lord Burlington. Kent's gothick is the quintessence of all this and to be laid under tribute must be the gothick of Wren at Christchurch, Oxford or Hawksmoor at the Knights of the Garter stalls in Westminster Abbey. In the early decades of the century it seems always to have been gothick by association, that is an addition in a gothick style to an earlier building. The only exception seems to have been a mysterious house in High Wycombe, Buckinghamshire, dated 1728 and incorporating ogee-headed windows in Kent's manner. Right at the beginning of his career as an architect from *c.* 1730, Kent designed in gothick, and with Esher Place, Surrey, Henry

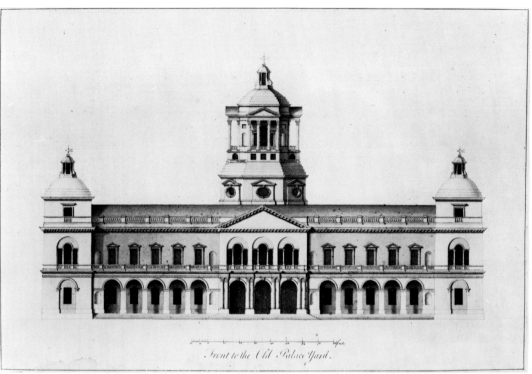

Front to the Old Palace Yard.

70

Pelham's enlargement *c.* 1732 of a Tudor tower that had been built by Wolsey, he created a model gothick country house that became a quarry throughout the century for dozens of gothick houses. An unexecuted but particularly apposite example of Kent's gothick is Honingham Hall, Norfolk, where he was asked in 1737 to titivate up and add wings to an East Anglian Elizabethan house. His proposed treatment was almost duplicated at Rousham House, Oxfordshire, when that 16th century house was remodelled by Kent from 1738.

70 Lord Burlington and William Kent *invenit*. Another *delin*. Elevation of the front to Old Palace Yard of a new Houses of Parliament at Westminster, London. Pen and wash (310 × 475)

71

71 William Kent. Elevation of the entrance front of Honingham Hall, Norfolk, 1737. Pen and wash (360 × 500)

72 John Vardy. Alternative elevations for a classic or gothick solution to rebuilding Milton Abbey, Dorset. Pen and wash (335 × 362)

At Milton Abbey in Dorset the 1st Lord Milton asked John Vardy for designs for a new house *c*. 1755. He was provided with alternative elevations, one gothick in association with the adjacent medieval abbey church. As a colleague of Kent's in the Office of Works, Vardy is here imitating his style. It is not insignificant that when Milton Abbey was rebuilt by Sir William Chambers in 1771, one facade was modelled upon Esher Place, hinting that Vardy's designs may also have drawn upon this source.

72

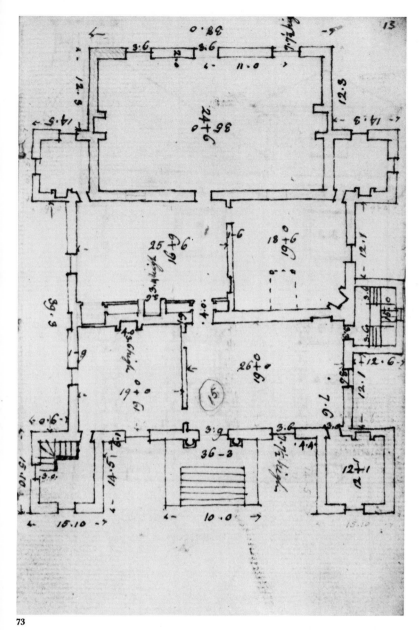

73

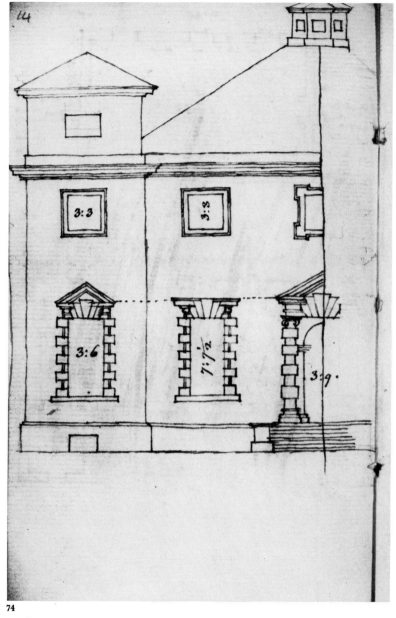

74

Kent either had no inclination to design a villa or was never given the opportunity. If Campbell pioneered and popularised the villa, its most innovative practitioner was Roger Morris who seems to have been closely linked with Campbell in the later 1720s. He developed an idiosyncratic style that may owe something to Lord Pembroke, for whom he acted as an amanuensis and affected a relationship similar to that between Burlington and Kent. Combe Bank (Figs 73–78) in Kent typifies his

villa style and was built in 1725 for Colonel John Campbell who later became 4th Duke of Argyll. He composes with great individuality, referring as much to Campbell, and Burlington, as to Palladio, but not blatantly derivative. In 1748 John Adam was sent from Scotland to England on a commission for the Duke and Morris for the Board of Ordnance. His sketch book contains sketches of Combe Bank as well as Morris's Whitton, another of his cubic villas.

73–77 Roger Morris *invenit*. John Adam *delin*. Details from travel sketchbook of Combe Bank, Kent. Pen, in book (160 × 100)

73 Plan of ground floor

74 Elevation of half entrance front

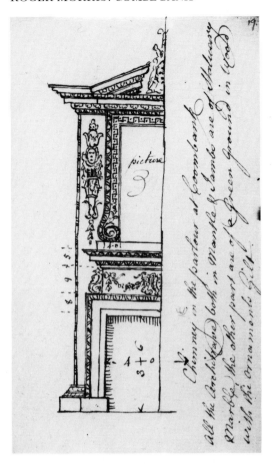

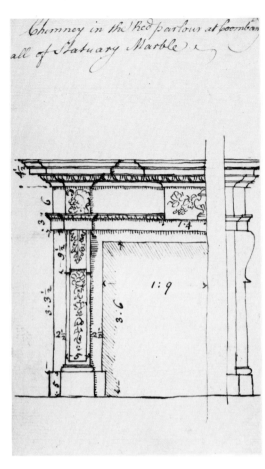

75 Elevation of half of the Parlour chimney piece

76 Elevation of tabernacle frame in vestibule

77 Half elevation and section of Red Parlour chimney piece

78 Detail of Combe Bank, Kent, from engraving by
William Woollett

Issac Ware and Henry Flitcroft represent the second generation of architects in training through the 1720s, in their case under Lord Burlington's patronage. Compared to Ware, Flitcroft is an architectural conservative, composing from established sources and models. His church of St Giles in the Fields, commissioned by the Vestry in 1731, is firmly in the Wren–Gibbs tradition and in fact borrows blatantly from Gibbs's St Martin's in the Fields, even to the galleried interior. This complete set of designs (Figs 79–84) is for the church with a cupola termination to the tower, whereas in the wooden model (and as executed) Flitcroft provided a tower with steeple, also from St Martin's.

79 Henry Flitcroft. Ground floor plan of St Giles in the Fields, London. Pen and wash (520 × 360)

80 Henry Flitcroft. Elevation of west front of St Giles in the Fields, London. Pen and wash (450 × 360)

81 Henry Flitcroft. Elevation of east end of St Giles in the Fields, London. Pen and wash (452 × 360)

82 Henry Flitcroft. North–south section of St Giles in the Fields, London. Pen and wash (422 × 355)

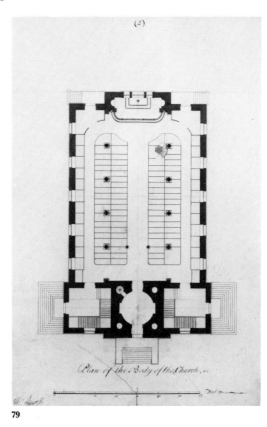

79

80

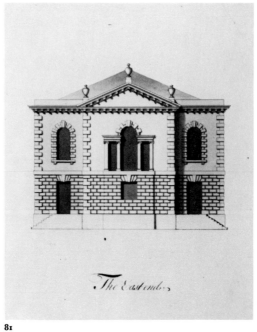

81

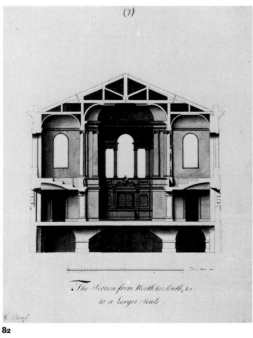

82

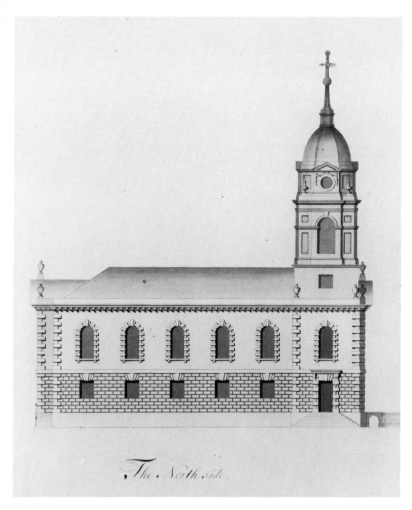

83 Henry Flitcroft. Elevation of north side of St Giles in the Fields, London. Pen and wash (520 × 430)

84 Henry Flitcroft. East–west section of St Giles in the Fields, London. Pen and wash (520 × 430)

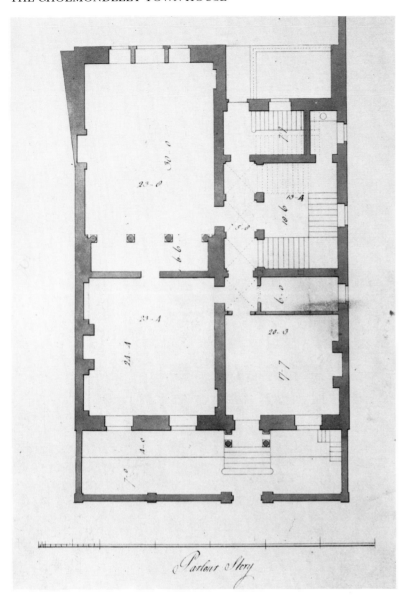

Parlour Story

The Cholmondeley House designs (Figs 85–91) comprise a rare and very complete set of drawings proposed for a London house around the middle years of the 18th century. The architect is unknown, but was someone of the status of Matthew Brettingham. The builder was the 3rd Earl of Cholmondeley, who clearly demanded of his architect much care and consultation in the preparation of designs. Not only has the architect provided plans and elevations of several schemes, but each room is represented by a plan with laid-out elevations of the walls. In addition there are designs for chimney-pieces and ceilings, and most interestingly the proposals by Gideon Gosset, carver and frame-maker of Berwick St, Soho, for arranging the paintings on the walls of the room (Fig. 92). Whoever the architect was, he had provided a simple, straight-forward plan that was of fairly common type. A porch led into a hall, a passage into a staircase, and to one side a front and back room, the latter with a columned screen and a Palladian window looking onto the garden. There is nothing affected here, just handsome finely-detailed and proportioned rooms for the display of pictures.

The time was not yet ripe for the feminist, overall linear decoration of Robert Adam to take control, with its innovative spatial arrangements.

85 Unidentified architect. Ground floor plan of Cholmondeley house

86 Unidentified architect. Entrance elevation of Cholmondeley house. Pen and wash (355 × 230)

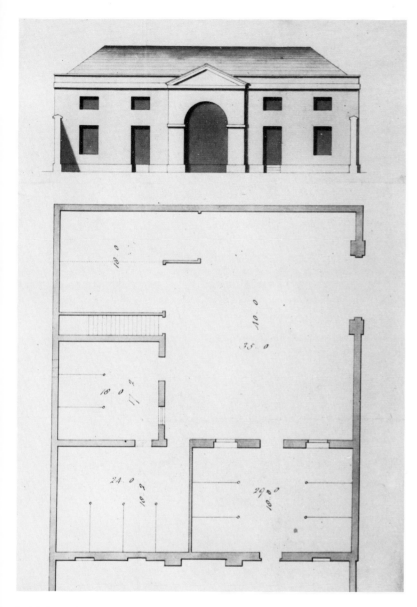

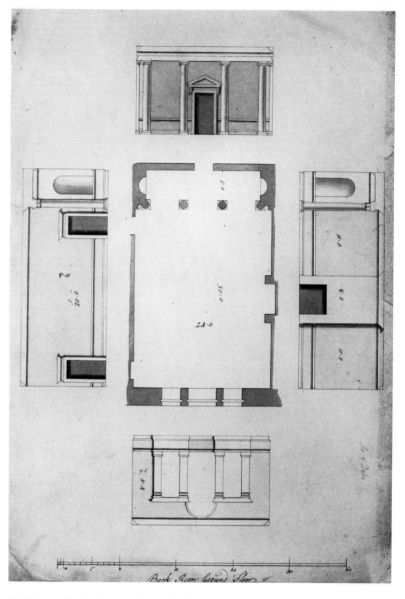

87 Unidentified architect. Plan of stables and elevation to garden of Cholmondeley house. Pen and wash (360 × 235)

88 Unidentified architect. Plan and laid-out wall elevations of Back Room, ground floor, of Cholmondeley house. Pen and wash (355 × 265)

89 Unidentified architect. Elevation of chimney piece in Back Bed Chamber, attic storey, of Cholmondeley house. Pen and wash (180 × 260)

90 Unidentified architect. Plan of a ceiling from an alternative project for Cholmondeley house. Pen and wash (300 × 200)

89

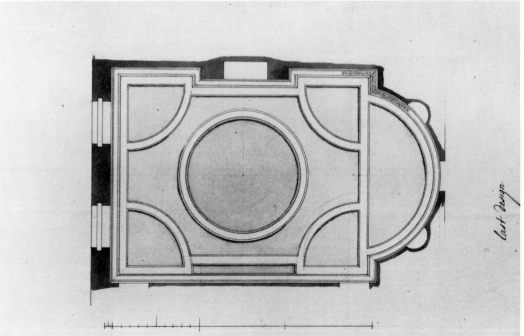

90

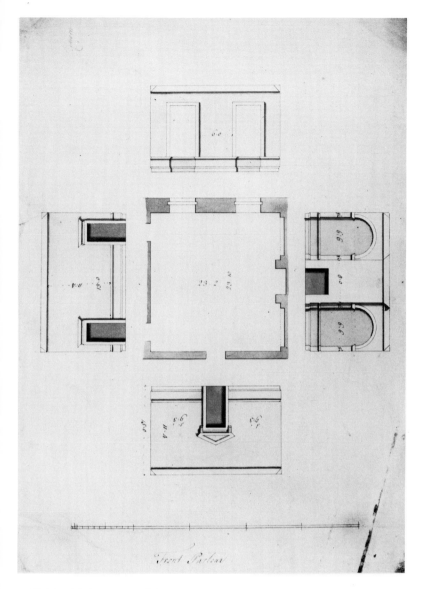

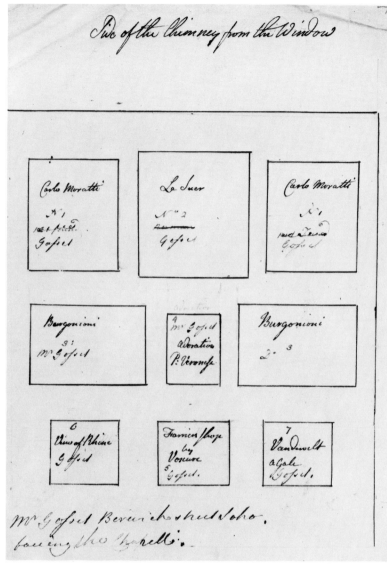

91 Unidentified architect. Plan and laid-out wall elevations of front Parlour of Cholmondeley house. Pen and wash (365 × 260)

92 Gideon Gosset. Wall plan showing method of arranging paintings, probably after framing by Gosset. Pen (370 × 235)

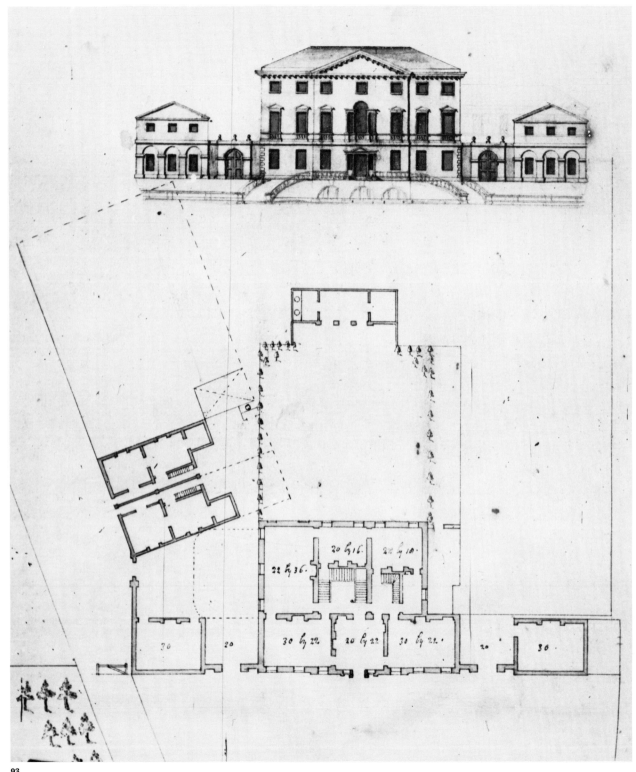

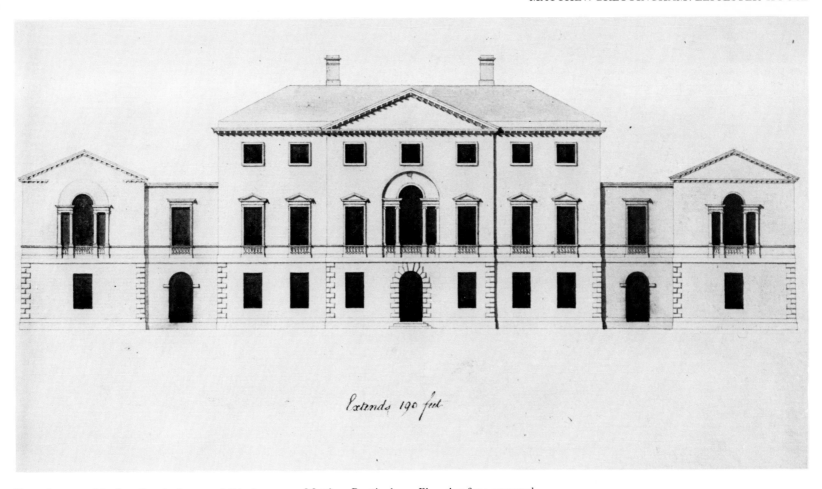

Extends 190 feet

From the 1740s Matthew Brettingham established a busy London practice, and designed grand town houses such as Norfolk House (1748), Egremont House (1756) and York House (1761). He, rather than Campbell or Burlington, established a type of utilitarian Palladian town house that fronted such thoroughfares as Piccadilly or squares as St James's (Figs 93–4). In the early 1740s Lord Leicester entertained ideas of building a grand town house in Berkeley Square, on the site where Robert Adam later began a house for Lord Bute in 1762, completing it as Lansdowne House in 1768. Brettingham always favoured an astylar elevation, usually in 2–3–2 bays with a pediment, and in planning he disposed his rooms in straightforward ways with no attempt at spatial incident.

93 Matthew Brettingham. Plan and elevation for proposed town house in Berkeley Square, London. Pen, pencil and wash (290 × 230)

94 Matthew Brettingham. Elevation for a proposed house in Berkeley Square, London. Pen and wash (270 × 370)

John Sanderson represents a Palladian who belongs
to the second generation. In 1731 he designed
Stratton Park, Hampshire, for the 3rd Duke of
Bedford, and this big house was, in terms of
elevation, a trial run for the 4th Duke's Woburn
Abbey designed by Flitcroft in 1747, for that was
nothing more than a recasting of Stratton. Working
drawings (Figs 95–6) suggest that Sanderson also
built a large rotunda house whose location has
never been established. As these came from Copped
Hall in Essex, they may all be preliminary studies
for that house, built by Sanderson for John Conyers
from 1753, but apparently under the direction of
others. Sanderson, however, seemed to have
frequently shown his designs around to various
clients to give an idea of the sort of house he was
capable of designing. He uses all the conventional
Palladian elements, but in a somewhat more refined
way than his contemporary Flitcroft. He was
certainly aware of prevailing fashions, as he was
adept at rococo decoration, and as his rotunda hall
decoration reveals (Fig. 155) was a fine and sensitive
draughtsman.

95 John Sanderson. Plan and elevation for a house
with a hexastyle portico and large circular rotunda-
type central hall. Pen and wash (515 × 360)

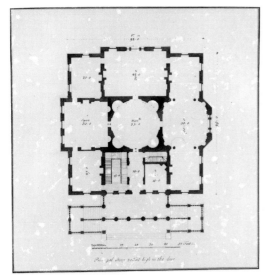

96 John Sanderson. Plan of a rotonda-type house with a dome and hexastyle portico. Pen and wash (300 × 285)

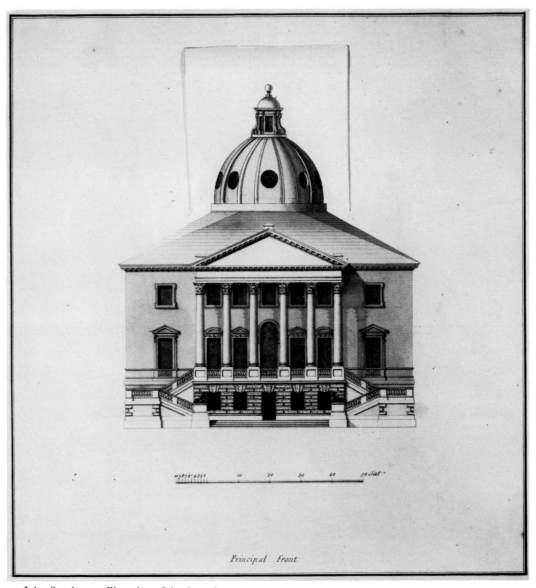

Principal Front

97 John Sanderson. Elevation of the domed rotonda-type house. Pen and wash (300 × 285) (*see also* Fig. 155)

98

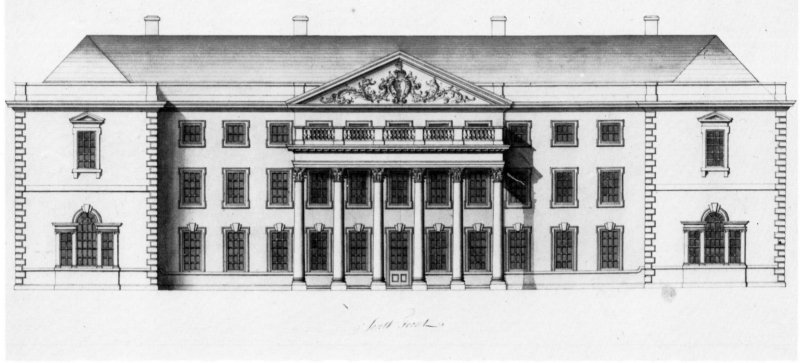

99

Whereas Flitcroft, Ware or Sanderson were metropolitan architects, representing a brand of Palladianism that was close to the source of Burlington's 'Rule of Taste', Palladianism in the provinces is not only secondhand in derivation, often transmitted through pattern books, but can be said to be tainted with provincial solecisms. Throughout the provinces families of architects established themselves in the county towns, and the Hiornes of Warwick were a typical firm of leading masons and architects. Both William and David

built Gopsall Hall, Leicestershire, for Charles Jennens about 1750–60 (Figs 98–9). Lack of clear articulation and clarity of composition reveals how such architects were unable to see a building both inside and outside in terms of proportions and the spacing of windows. John Westley, the carpenter, who designed Gopsall has looked at James Gibbs's *Book of Architecture*, 1728, and mis-mashed what he found there with a variety of ideas from other pattern books and extant houses. The stables, in contrast, are in correct taste, and by the competent Hiornes.

98 William and David Hiorne (or Hiorns). Elevation of the north front of Gopsall Hall, Leicestershire. Pen and wash (245 × 725)

99 William and David Hiorne. Elevation of the south front of Gopsall Hall, Leicestershire. Pen and wash (240 × 475)

The SOUTH Front of HORTON HOUSE. belonging to the EARL of Hallifax

Although Colen Campbell had tried to attract the 1st Earl of Halifax's patronage in 1715 with a grand design for a country house, presumably for rebuilding the old family seat at Horton in Northamptonshire, his inveigling came to nought despite describing Halifax in his preface as 'the great Maecenas' of his age. It was left to the 2nd Earl to rebuild Horton, and this was a piece-meal affair, seemingly a progressive refacing of the fronts. The 1st Earl may have employed Daniel Garrett for one front, and this was frankly sub-standard. When it came to the south front the 2nd Earl had become attracted to an amateur architect and astronomer called Thomas Wright who designed the south front about 1753 (Fig. 100). At Horton Wright was forced

to compromise and draw an elevation conforming to the old house. Projecting rounded or segmental bays were his speciality, in this case rising the height of the front to terminate in shallow domes. The huge hexastyle portico, in association with the dome, adds a hint of grandeur. Wright's interiors were nearly always lavishly rococo.

100 Unidentified topographer *delin*. Thomas Wright *invenit*. Elevation of the south front of Horton House, Northamptonshire. Pen and wash (320 × 435)

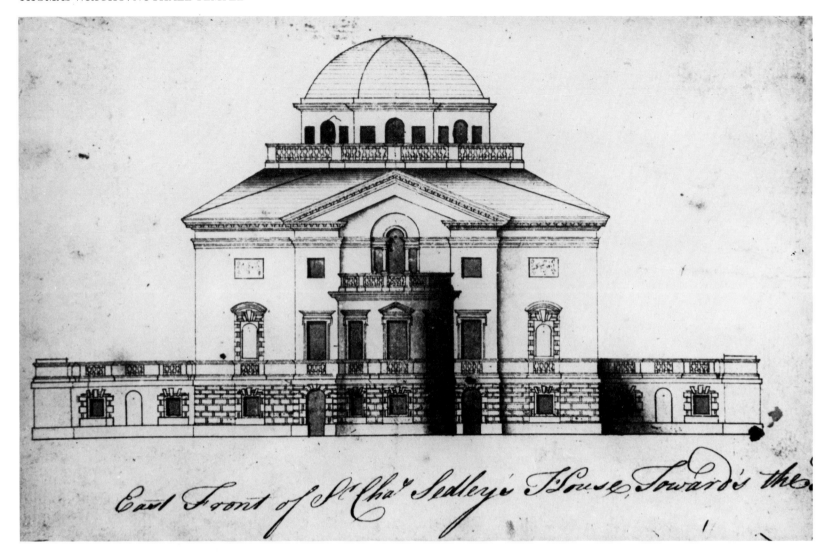

East Front of Sr Char Sedley's House, Towards the

Nuthall Temple in Nottinghamshire, built for Sir Charles Sedley from 1754, was one of the most spectacular of all the rotunda villas. Wright was able to build a complete house *de novo* to his taste (Fig. 101). His attitude to composition, being that of an amateur, was less trammelled by precedent than would have been the case with a professional architect. Nuthall is Burlingtonian, and possessed an octagonal hall, adorned with rich plasterwork, that, before its destruction in 1929, could claim to be one of the most beautiful surviving rooms of the whole Georgian period.

101 Unidentified topographer *delin*. Thomas Wright *invenit*. Elevation of the east front of Nuthall Temple, Nottinghamshire. Pen and wash (145 × 215)

In contrast to the metropolitan, but nevertheless derivative suavity of Flitcroft's St Giles in the Fields, William Halfpenny's design for the Protestant Cathedral at Waterford in Ireland (Fig. 102) is purely rustic, or Palladian vernacular. It was submitted in 1739 but never built and it fairly represents a builder's misunderstanding of Palladianism. As the compiler of many pattern books on architecture, Halfpenny might have been expected to have designed something a little more sophisticated. In most rural areas and in country towns this was the extent to which local builders acknowledged Burlington's Rule of Taste. Halfpenny's links with Ireland were probably through his residence in Bristol, from which town he issued his *Perspective Made Easy* in 1731. From 1722 he published or contributed to over 24 books, and was with Batty Langley the most prolific architectural propagandist and educator of the mid-century.

Concurrently with his involvement at Waterford, Halfpenny seemingly prepared a number of designs for small houses (unless they were made for Bristol at the same time). One drawing (Fig. 103) is signed and dated 1739 and inscribed to the effect that it 'may be executed for 1400 pounds'. To describe these (Figs 103–4 *overleaf*) as Palladian would cause Palladio distress, but they employ in a vernacular manner Gibbsian doorways and voussoired windows that in England ultimately derive from the Whitehall designs in Kent's *Inigo Jones*. They are symptomatic of much Anglo-Irish Palladianism, although the extent of Halfpenny's intervention on the Irish scene has never been assessed, because of the lack of documentation.

102 William Halfpenny. Plan and elevation of north front and two alternative proposals for the termination of the tower, for the Protestant Cathedral in Waterford, Ireland. Pen and wash (422 × 235)

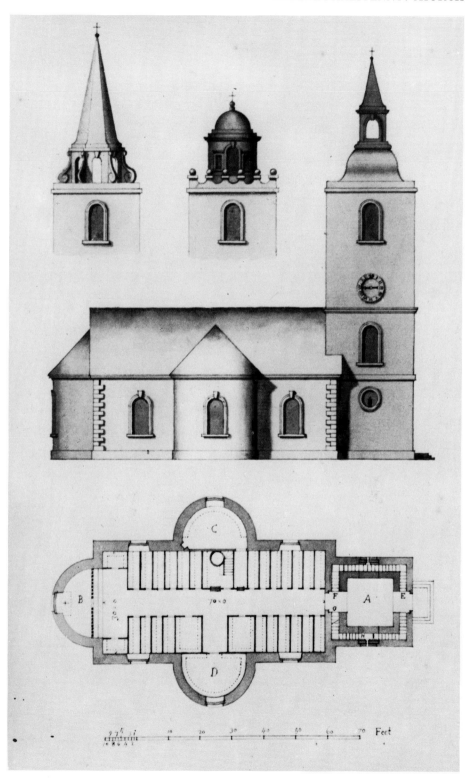

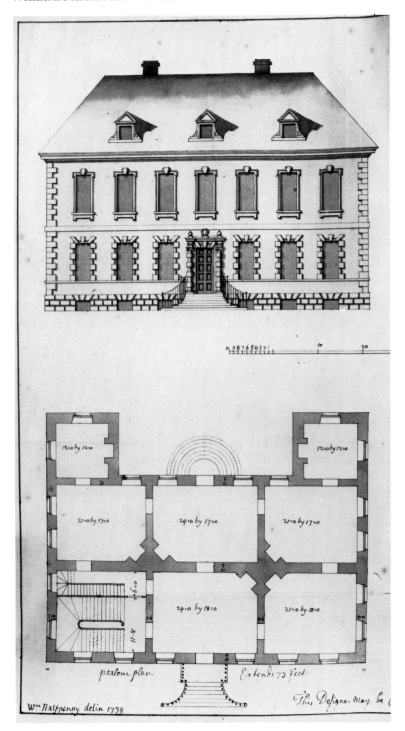

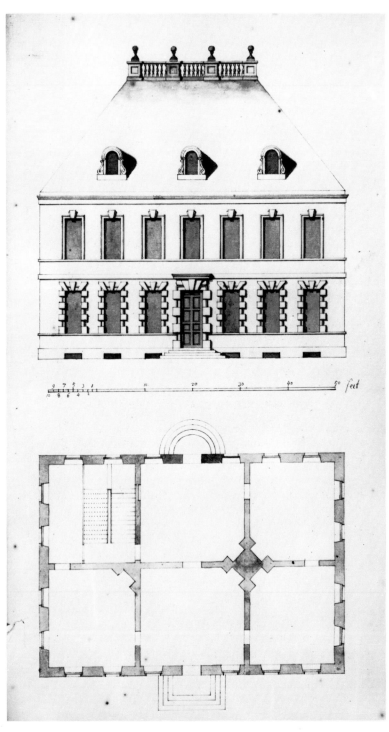

103 William Halfpenny. Plan and elevation for a house costing 1400 pounds, perhaps for Waterford, Ireland. Pen and wash (420 × 240)

104 William Halfpenny. Plan and elevation of a house, perhaps for Waterford, Ireland. Pen and wash (420 × 240)

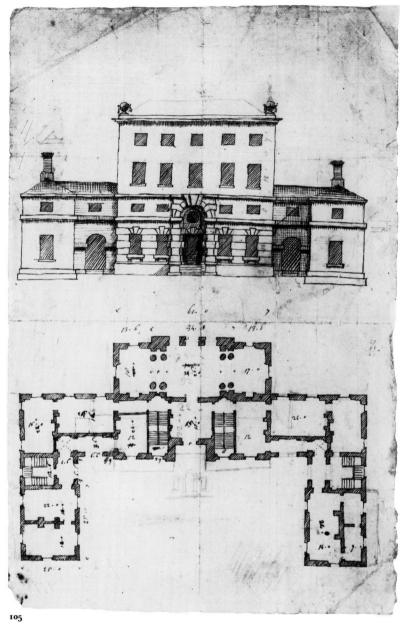

105

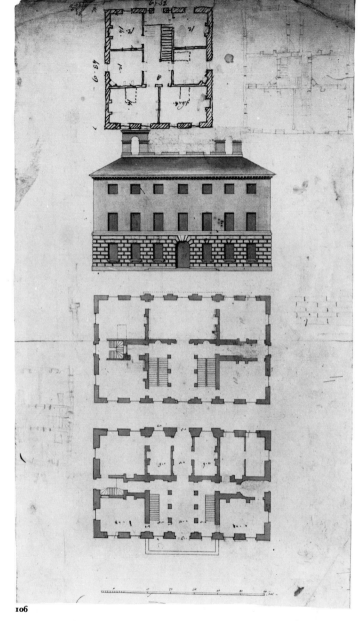

106

In Sir Edward Lovett Pearce Ireland possessed a
Palladian architect who for distinction stands with
Burlington and Kent. He was almost certainly
trained by his relation Vanbrugh and studied
Palladio's architecture in Italy in 1723. The Dublin
Parliament House is a building of major importance
and belongs to a small group of distinguished works
built between 1726 and Pearce's early death in
1733. Burlington's dry, academic neo-Palladianism
did not appeal to him, and his connection with

Vanbrugh imbues his plans and elevations with a
more sculptural and spatial quality. The two
designs reproduced here (Figs 105–6) are for
unidentified projects, and both display
Vanbrughian influences, one with heavy string
courses and deep baroque porch, the other with
arcaded chimney stacks and stairs screened from the
hall as in Vanbrugh's Grimsthorpe Castle.

105 Sir Edward Lovett Pearce. Plan and elevation
for a small house with wings. Pen and pencil
(390 × 260)

106 Sir Edward Lovett Pearce. Two floor plans and
elevation for a large six bay house, and rough
studies for the plan of a smaller house. Pen, pencil
and wash (422 × 242)

JOHN WOOD THE ELDER: HOUSE IN BATH

In a city like Bath neo-Palladianism and neo-classicism cover a continuous story of development under John Wood the elder (died 1754) and John Wood the younger (died 1781). It is Wood the elder who begins to apply a Palladian canon to the urban look of the city, at Queen's Square from 1729, North and South Parades from 1740, and, in his last work, The Circus from 1754, completed by his son. Wood was also the architect of Ralph Allen's great mansion of Prior Park from 1735, and here he used Campbell's Wanstead I as a model. Wood was also a publicist, and his *Essay towards a Description of Bath* in 1742 contained engravings of his buildings, as did his *Description of the Exchange at Bristol* in 1745. Much of Wood's building remains unidentified, for he must have been busily employed on utilitarian street frontages that bear no distinctive stylistic marks. This is the case with this plan and elevation (Figs 107–8) for a combination of shop and dwelling that may have been proposed on a frontage east of the Abbey church near the King's and Queen's Baths.

107 John Wood the elder (attributed to). Plan of a merchant's house in Bath, Somerset. Pen and wash (230 × 350)

108 John Wood the elder (attributed to). Elevation of sloping street front to a merchant's house in Bath, Somerset. Pen and wash (230 × 350)

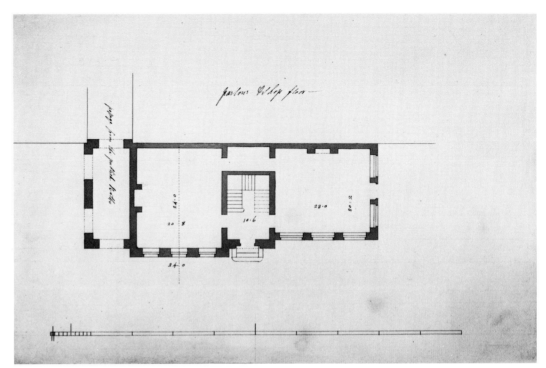

107

108

The three designs on this page (Figs 109–11) are selected as arbitrary models. The long section drawn in fine pen is through a very large Palladian tower house with wings of the Holkham type containing all the mannerisms of Kent's staccato style such as recess and advancing of planes, screen walls topped with balls, and Chiswick-type Palladian windows set in a relieving arch. The architect is unknown, but must be someone connected to the Office of Works and undoubtedly a Palladian of the second generation. Also, the provincial and somewhat dull design for a house with an attached tetrastyle portico is by Michael Wills who signs an album of designs 'Dublin 9 May 1745' and describes them as 'Vitruvian Designs in the oeconomic style'. This particular house was costed at £7541.2.0. The provenance of the drawing for the five bay house with the line-up of Palladian motifs in its centre or entrance bay, was with some Midland designs associated with John Carr. A rusticated doorway combined with a Palladian window above and, above that, a Diocletian window, became a fashionable way to add some aggrandisement to a town house. Such a one, for example, exists in Lincoln, and although this particular drawing is not in Henry Flitcroft's hand, the elevation closely resembles his Stivichall Hall, Warwickshire, built for Arthur Gregory in 1755 and now demolished.

109 Unidentified architect. Section through a great Palladian house of Holkham type. Pen (310 × 530)

110 Michael Wills. Elevation for grand house costing £7541.2.0. for Ireland, 1745. Pen and wash (380 × 540)

111 Unidentified architect. Elevation of a house similar to Flitcroft's Stivichall, Warwickshire. Pen (490 × 380)

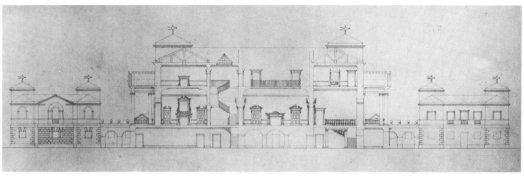

109

110

111

The two washed-in elevations (Figs 112-13) are
attributed to William Paty (1758–1800) and are for
a new house, or a rebuilding, of Butleigh Court,
Somerset, for James Garrick. They can hardly be
dated before the 1780s and therefore show how
conservative, and frankly dull, provincial architects
from centres such as Bristol could be.

112 William Paty. Elevation for rebuilding Butleigh
Court, Somerset. Pen and wash (265 × 450)

113 William Paty. Alternative elevation for
rebuilding Butleigh Court, Somerset. Pen and wash
(265 × 450)

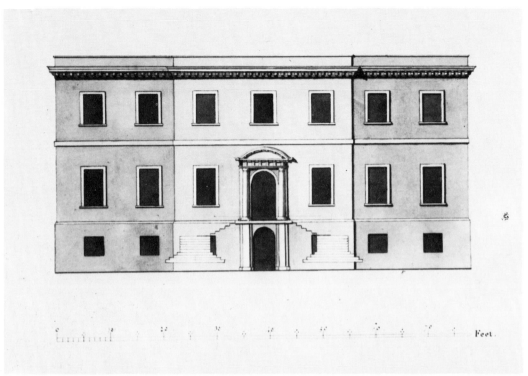

112

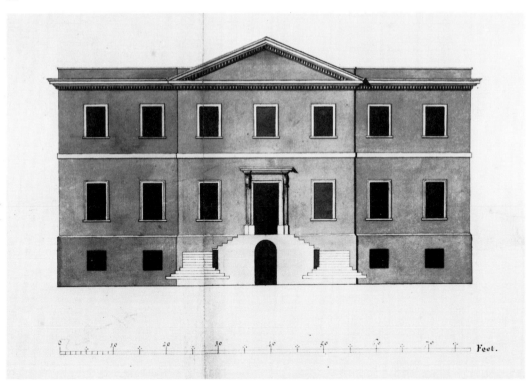

113

The other pair of designs (Figs 114–15) are both for the same house, and here the unknown architect, for an unknown client, at an unknown situation, has proposed two solutions, two years apart in 1754 and 1756. This is Palladianism by one of the John Sanderson sort. The 1756 design with its massive cornices and projections and centres and angles would have demanded far more expensive stonework than the chaster, smaller design of 1754.

114 Unidentified architect. Elevation for the east front of a large country house, 1756. Pen and pencil (240 × 380)

115 Unidentified architect. Elevation for the west front of a country house, 1754. Pen and pencil (240 × 380)

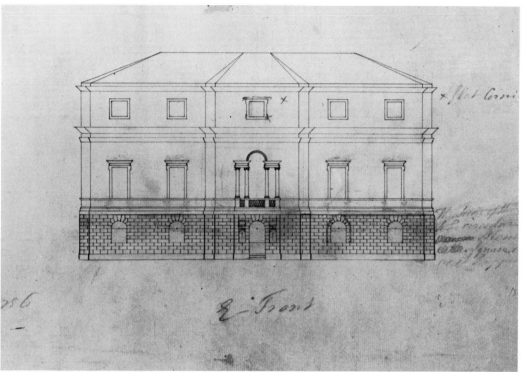

114

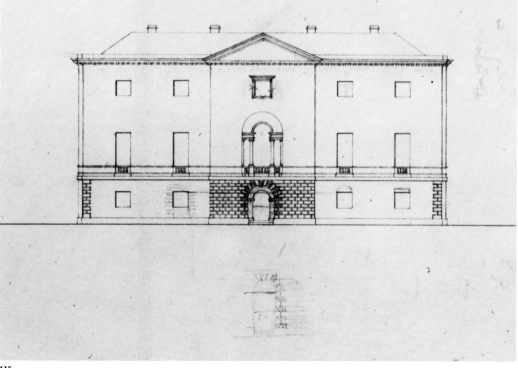

115

116

117

Ambrose Phillips of Garendon (*c.* 1707–1737) was one of the most serious-minded of amateurs. After inheriting Garendon in Leicestershire he travelled extensively in France and Italy making detailed and competent studies of architecture, especially Roman buildings in the south of France. Although these two designs (Figs 116–17) were proposed for building around the Place Royale du Peyrou in Montpellier, they later provided Phillips with the basic programme for his new house, begun about

1735. In elevation this was not unlike the plainness of Wood's Prior Park – almost utilitarian in the absence of carved detail. Phillips was significantly one of the first members of the Society of Dilettanti, founded between 1732 and 1734.

116 Ambrose Phillips. Section through project for Place Royale du Peyrou, Montpellier, France, showing elevations of ends of courtyard wings and front of porticoed temple or church. Pen and wash (175 × 370)

117 Ambrose Phillips. Elevation of main front of courtyard blocks to Place Royale du Peyrou, Montpellier, France. Pen and wash (165 × 330)

Like Ambrose Phillips, Sir George Gray (died 1773) was one of the founding members of the Society of Dilettanti, and its secretary and treasurer from 1739 until 1771. Gray's role in the designing of Spencer House, Green Park, London, has never been assessed, for although it was built by John Vardy for the 1st Earl Spencer from 1756 to 1765, Gray seems to have approved all the designs. It must have been Gray who encouraged Spencer to employ James Stuart in the house from 1759 and at Wimbledon Park, Surrey, somewhat earlier; but this concerns the early history of neoclassicism. Gray's design (Fig. 118) for the 'peers & Gate' at Lord Cadogan's Caversham Park, Oxfordshire, is conventionally Palladian, in the manner of Kent. Robert Hampden Trevor was in contrast to Phillips and Gray an amateur of very decided scholarly attainment, being a fine latinist. His architectural drawings are likewise learned, composed and drawn with much drafting skill. His proposal (Fig. 119) here is for a pentagon-shaped house, following a trend for centralised buildings that pre-occupied Palladians such as Timothy Lightoler and Theodore Jacobsen.

118 Sir George Gray. Plan and elevations for gate piers at Caversham Park, Oxfordshire. Pen and wash (300 × 420)

119 Robert Hampden Trevor. Plan of a pentagon-shaped house with circular towers. Pen, pencil and wash (270 × 380)

118

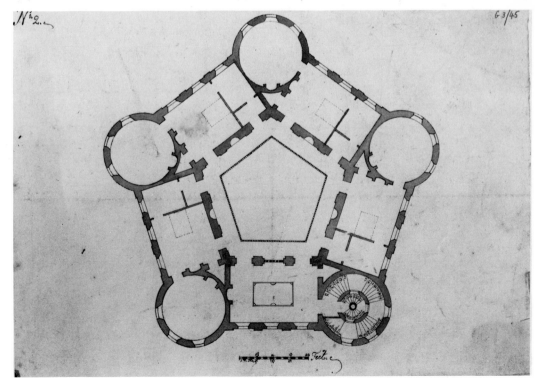

119

120

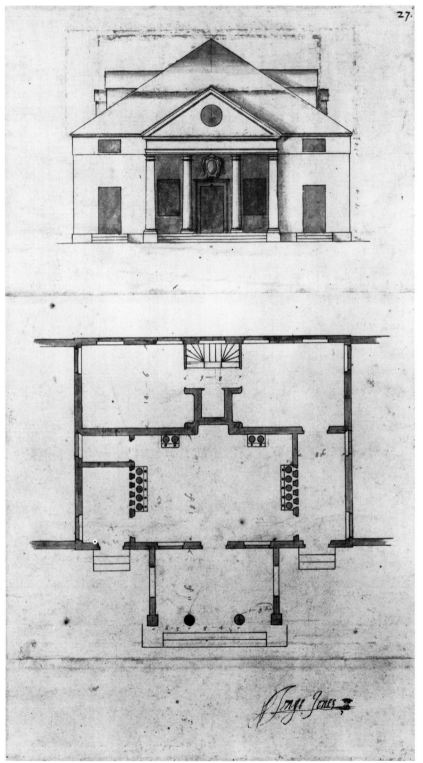

27.

Inigo Jones never designed a garden temple, for in
the early years of the 17th century the Italianate
temple garden had not yet been introduced to
England. Temples appear in some of his masque
designs, but were never translated into real
existence in a garden. It is quite another matter
with utilitarian buildings such as stables, brew
houses, garden gateways or hunting lodges. At
Newmarket Palace soon after he was appointed
Surveyor General of the King's Works in September
1615, he first built a brew house, stable, dog-house
and riding house and then shortly afterwards the
new Prince's Lodging for Charles, Prince of Wales,
together with a Clerk of Works's house. These two
designs (Figs 120–21) are presumably for a brew
house and for either a stable or dog-house. As the
style of the draughtsmanship of the latter is early,
and as the former is early by virtue of his signature
(never seen on drawings after about 1620), both
may be for Newmarket. The brew house (Fig. 121)
is Scamozzian, leaning upon a design in Scamozzi's
book of 1616. The dog-house, if it is such, is almost
like a prop out of a masque, drawn with a delicacy
of line and wash characteristic of masque drawings.
It has a rusticity that seems appropriate for a
utilitarian building in the country.

120 Inigo Jones. Elevation for a stable, perhaps for
Newmarket Palace, Suffolk. Pen and watercolour
(380 × 215)

121 Inigo Jones. Plan and elevation for a brew
house, perhaps for Newmarket Palace, Suffolk. Pen
and wash (320 × 410)

121

122

123

Even if he was not inventive, Campbell was innovative, and his scheme of things embraced not only the great house, the villa and the town house, but gardens too. Not enough is known about the exact role he played in garden design, but Ebberston in 1718, in Yorkshire, and Hall Barn, Buckinghamshire in 1724 had important gardens to which no name of a garden designer has been attributed. At Chiswick, Campbell may have partnered Burlington in the laying-out of the basons of water with their temples, admittedly designed by Burlington, and it may have been Campbell who

proposed temples as the terminating points of the avenues before 1718. Some of his temples are villas in miniature, and these two designs (Figs 122–3) draw upon the same vocabulary of voussoired and rusticated doorways and windows. The motifs tend to be repetitive, but Campbell always displays bravura and panache in his treatment of bold elements.

122 Colen Campbell. Elevation for a garden pavilion with cupola. Pen and wash (450 × 310)

123 Colen Campbell. Elevation for a garden pavilion with pediment and Ionic pilasters. Pen and wash (365 × 235)

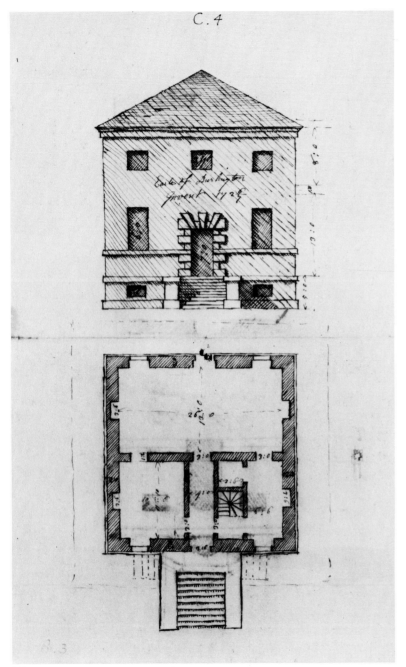

124

125

124 Lord Burlington. Plan and elevation for Round
Coppice, Buckinghamshire, 1727. Pen (312 × 195)

125 Lord Burlington *invenit*. Henry Flitcroft *delin*.
Plan and elevation for the pavilion near the lake,
Chiswick House, London. Pen and wash (180 × 230)

One of the most delightful of all miniature neo-Palladian lodges was that built for Lord Bruce at Round Coppice near Iver, Buckinghamshire. Bruce obtained designs from his brother-in-law Burlington (Fig. 124) for a house conveniently situated near the road from London to Marlborough. The exact form of the lodge as built is not certain for it was demolished in 1954 without record.

Lord Burlington's first garden building was his own Casina or Bagnio terminating one of the avenues and built in 1717. Although Campbell ascribes this to Burlington in *Vitruvius Britannicus* it may well have been drawn up by Campbell himself. The earliest garden buildings from his lordship's hand date to the first years of the 1720s. Around two basons of water east of the old long canal Burlington built the domed Orange Tree Garden temple and this Tuscan temple (Fig. 125) with a portico derived from the same Scamozzi model as Jones's Newmarket Brew House one.

Mereworth Castle today can be seen as an aesthetically satisfying composition where the porticoes of the villa are answered by those of the flanking office pavilions. These latter, however, were not built until about 1740, possibly by Roger Morris. Campbell's villa was flanked on one side by this office and stable block, signed and dated in the drawing 1723 (Figs 126–7).

Despite Campbell's activity in making designs for the 2nd Duke of Richmond at Goodwood in Sussex, nothing was apparently built. The death of the 1st Duke in 1723 seemed to have inspired a profusion of designs, for a huge new neo-Palladian house, and, in a small scale, this drawing (Fig. 128) for 'some distant offices at Goodwood 1724'. This was the period of Roger Morris's involvement with Campbell and he seems to have ingratiated himself with the Duke in a way that Campbell could not.

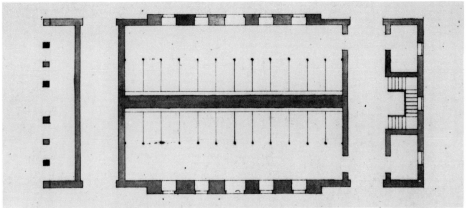

126

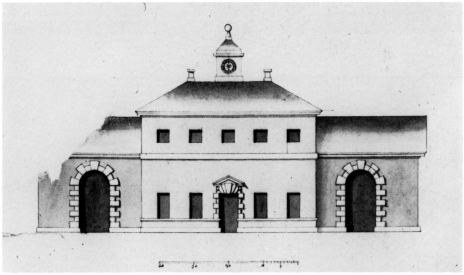

127

126 Colen Campbell. Plan of offices at Mereworth Castle, Kent, 1723. Pen and wash (410 × 240)

127 Colen Campbell. Elevation for offices at Mereworth Castle, Kent, 1723. Pen and wash (410 × 240)

128 Colen Campbell. Elevation for 'distant offices' at Goodwood House, Sussex, 1724. Pen and wash (410 × 225)

128

Both John Sanderson's design (Fig. 129) for a stable complex and the Hiornes' elevation for stables at Gopsall in Leicestershire (Fig. 130), show the form stables were assuming around the middle years of the century. Sanderson's is more traditionally Palladian, with Kentian or Burlingtonian towers and a fully rusticated central archway. Both employ the device of the Diocletian window to light the stalls, an idea that took hold from the late 1720s, Campbell having used them at Houghton by 1726. Hiornes' Gopsall work can be dated in the late 1750s and early 1760s.

The Gopsall Collection represents a very remarkable survival of a group of designs (Figs 130–1, also 98–99) made for a country house, both inside and outside, as well as for all those accompaniments that find a place in the garden. In many ways the designs, however varied they might be, are typical of a Palladian house in Georgian England. Those who worked for Charles Jennens, John Westley, William Hiorne or James Paine, and other unidentified architects, builders and decorators, may not have created houses as great as Chiswick or Houghton, but their buildings are more typical of the mean. The Gopsall designs are notable for the attention given to garden works, temples, bath houses, bowling greens, seats, and in the case of this drawing (Fig. 131) the essential greenhouse, proposed here by William and David Hiorne. Greenhouses had still not yet developed beyond their form in the late 17th century, with a frontally-lit building, often temple-like, for the protection of orange trees and delicate plants, and lean-to glazed hot houses with stoves for, as Hiorne inscribes, 'young plants' and 'Fruit'.

129 John Sanderson. Elevation for stables. Pen and wash (440 × 230)

130 William and David Hiorne. Elevation for proposed stables at Gopsall Hall, Leicestershire. Pen and wash (172 × 362)

131 William and David Hiorne. Plan, elevation and sections of the Greenhouse at Gopsall Hall, Leicestershire. Pen and wash (310 × 495)

129

130

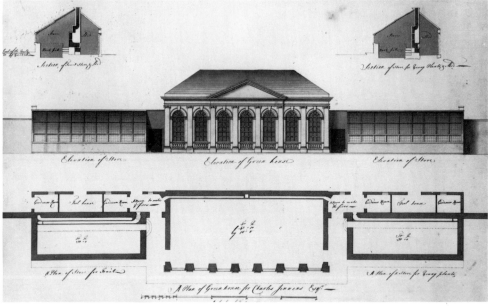

131

132

These two Palladian entrances (Figs 132–3) represent polarities of individual status, although not necessarily of architectural competence. One proposes a grand stair approach to a doorway onto a terrace, which can be identified as Queen Caroline's terrace at Windsor Castle, Berkshire, proposed by Lord Burlington in 1729, and drawn by Stephen Wright. The gateway itself resembles Inigo Jones's gate at Oatlands engraved by John Vardy in *Some Designs of Inigo Jones and Mr William Kent*, 1744. The other entrance takes us to the provincial world of Trowbridge in Wiltshire, for Esau Reynolds (1725–1778) was a builder and architect there. As the house is hypothetical, so is the gate entrance, grand perhaps, but not so smoothly absurd as the other design.

132 Esau Reynolds. Perspective of a proposed gateway to a Palladian house, 1748. Pen and wash (310 × 500)

133 Lord Burlington *invenit*. Stephen Wright *delin*. Plan and elevation for a grand gateway in the Oatlands Palace style, set upon a terrace for Windsor Castle, Berkshire, 1729. Pen and wash (330 × 520)

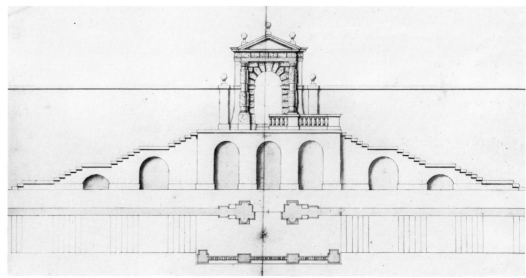

133

134

In these two temples a span of some forty years in
neo-Palladian England is covered. The closed
temple on a square plan (Fig. 134) is almost baroque
in its sculptural treatment of surfaces, and it takes
its cue from the elevation of pavilions on the
Whitehall designs as published by Kent in 1727.
The 'Open Temple' (Fig. 135) is more of a temple
proper, for when James Paine built it for Charles
Jennens at Gopsall about 1764 it was intended to
house Louis-Francois Roubiliac's statue of Religion.
Paine was a second generation Palladian who came
to terms with the neoclassicism of Chambers and
Adam after the 1760s.

134 Unidentified architect. Plan and elevation of a
garden temple. Pen and wash (220 × 180)

135 James Paine. Perspective of the Open Temple
for Gopsall Hall, Leicestershire. Pen and wash
(365 × 260)

135

Elevation of an Open Temple design'd for Jennings Esq.

Ja. Paine Arch. inv.t et Delin.t

Inigo Jones's interior style is unknown before 1619, the year he began the Banqueting House. No doubt his decorative vocabulary, then as afterwards, was based upon precedents in Palladio's *Four Books of Architecture* of 1570. This was his manual of the decorative part of civil architecture. The pages of Palladio can be turned and the model found for almost every detail in Jones's interiors. For the Queen's Chapel at St James's (Fig. 136) his elliptical coffered ceiling, 56 feet in length, is based upon the Temple of the Sun and Moon, its length of 56 *piedi* being simply transposed into English feet. The Queen's Chapel was a work of urgency, ordered in April 1623 with foundation stone laid less than a month later. Seen as the inspiration for so many 18th century Georgian churches, the Chapel was perhaps more important as a model than the Banqueting House. The narrow street facade is a rendition of the centre of the Prince's Lodging, but it is idle to speculate whether behind that Newmarket facade there was a saloon with a similar coffered ceiling. The most innovative part of the Queen's Chapel was the Venetian or Palladian window set in the east end, the precursor of countless others in Georgian churches. The chimney-piece in the Closet is another matter, for on the whole chimney-pieces are an element of northern necessity, and throughout his career Jones turned to French sources, although in this particular case Jones has opened his Scamozzi to find the chimney surround in the 'Aspetto della Nappa alla Veneziana'. This section was drawn by Henry Flitcroft for Lord Burlington, who may have contemplated having it engraved.

The Somerset House Chapel, installed by Jones in Queen Henrietta Maria's palace in 1630 was demolished with great melancholy by Sir William Chambers in 1776. The Chapel and the state apartments decorated by Jones (as well as by Kent in the following century) are a tragic loss. This measured drawing of the Chapel ceiling (Fig. 137) was, like that of the St James's Chapel, possibly prepared for publication. Jones's sources are here more eclectic, drawing upon Serlio for the octagonal coffering of the Closet, the wave moulding in the frieze and the interlocking 'S' scroll decoration on the beams of the ceiling. The compartition of the ceiling is like one in the Queen's House, for which designs were being made soon after 1630.

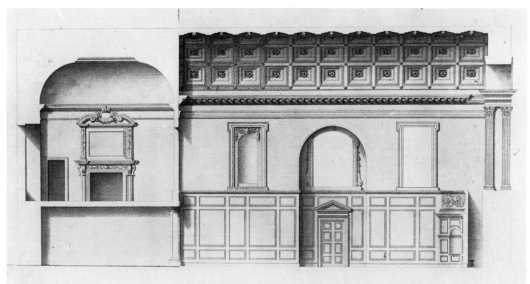

136

137

136 Inigo Jones *invenit*. Henry Flitcroft *delin*. Longitudinal, east–west, section through the Queen's Chapel, St James's Palace, London. Pen and wash (350 × 520)

137 Inigo Jones *invenit*. Henry Flitcroft *delin*. Plan of the ceiling, and section showing detail of cornice, of the Chapel, Somerset House, London. Pen and wash (350 × 520)

138

139

Somerset House may indicate a trend by Jones towards a greater eclecticism in his sources. The Chapel itself, although with a ceiling based upon Serlio, possessed a screen composed of curious pseudo-Jacobethan pilasters combined with pediments of the so-called 'Swan's Neck' or open scrolled variety. This is the first recorded instance of such pediments, that were to be universally used after the Restoration, and by William Kent in a decorative context after the late 1720s. The screen is, in fact, mannerist, in the same way that many of the effects in Jones's masque designs can be so called. In contrast, for the triglyphs of the entablature of his screen, Jones substituted scrolls based upon an antique fragment of marble at Arundel House. As Sir John Summerson has succinctly written, it is this 'interweaving of neo-classical and Mannerist thought' that is so striking about the Chapel. Due to our ignorance of the other interiors, much must remain guesswork, but descriptions evoke a type of richly ornamented interior, now lost to us. A most elegant design, for a door to the Queen's Cabinet, 1628–30, does survive (Fig. 139): it was used by Lord Burlington as a model for the doors at Chiswick.

138 Inigo Jones. Elevation of the window of the Chapel, Somerset House, London, 1632. Pen and pencil (280 × 450)

139 Inigo Jones. Elevation of the doorway to the Queen's Cabinet, Somerset House, London. Pen and pencil (320 × 290)

What remains in the Queen's House – and it is not very much – is the sole surviving evidence for Jones's interior style in the 1630s. Even in Lord Burlington's day nothing more survived, but even so, what there was, for example ceilings, balustrades, cornices and a variety of details, profoundly affected the vocabulary of neo-Palladian decoration. There is not a shred of evidence that any part of the Queen's House as completed from 1629 onwards for Queen Henrietta Maria was carried out from designs made in 1616. For a creatively evolving artist like Jones this would have been unthinkable. The most surprising incursion in the Queen's House programme is the French connection, for not only are several of Jones's designs for chimney-pieces (Fig. 140) based upon the engraved chimney-pieces in Barbet's *Livre d'Architecture* of 1633, but others are renditions of designs supplied by an unknown French architect to the Queen, who was, of course, French. It will probably never be known whether the Queen felt that she had allegiances to her compatriots, but whatever the reasons for compelling Jones to redraw (and improve) a French design, their effect was perhaps even stronger in the 18th century than in his own day, for Lord Burlington used them as models for Chiswick, and they were disseminated in the engraved works of William Kent, John Vardy and Isaac Ware.

140 Inigo Jones. Study for a chimney-piece in the Queen's House, Greenwich, London. Pen (190 × 290)

142

As with his country houses, it is really John Webb who acts as the bridge between Jones and the neo-Palladians, and in so many instances the latter found Webb's own designs more to their taste. Gunnersbury, Amesbury, the Queen's Gallery at Somerset House, interiors at Wilton and at Northumberland House, must all have provided a canon of Palladian or Jonesian design far more accessible than anything by Jones himself. These three designs (Figs 141–3) are for a variety of decorative and ornamental commissions: a chimney-piece in the bedroom at Drayton Park, Northamptonshire, designed for the 2nd Earl of Peterborough in 1653; the cartouche above the great Door in the Double Cube Room at Wilton, dated 1649 and done for the 4th Earl of Pembroke; and the cornice for the King's Bedchamber in the Charles II wing at Greenwich, made in 1666 but never executed (Fig. 143). But Webb remained unsung as a contributor to Burlington's 'Rule of Taste', just as Scamozzi never featured large in accounts of Jonesian Palladianism.

141 John Webb. Elevation of the chimney-piece in the Bedchamber, Drayton Park, Northamptonshire, 1653. Pen, pencil and wash (355 × 235)

142 John Webb. Study for the cartouche over the Great Door in the Double Cube Rome, Wilton House, Wiltshire, 1649. Pen and watercolour (200 × 170)

141

Very clearly there was a mild battle of the styles after the Restoration. Webb had hoped for and deserved the reversion of Surveyor General of the King's Works. It was not to be and Sir John Denham, an amateur, got the job, and even when Denham died in 1669 it was Wren who succeeded him. The truth was that Jones's Palladianism was out of fashion. The taste was for a Franco-Dutch infiltrated style that drew from sources in Italy other than Palladio's. The up-and-coming architects were Hugh May and Sir Christopher Wren. It must have been a bitter disappointment to Webb to have been commanded to design a royal palace at Greenwich and see it abandoned in 1669, five years after it was begun. All that was built was the west wing, now known as the Charles II Block, and even this was not completed to Webb's interior designs. Because Webb was forgotten and no one could distinguish between a drawing by Jones and one by Webb, all Webb's buildings were consigned to Jones, irrespective of the fact that many were built years after Jones's death. Webb's approach to both his architecture and his drafting method was academic, as is well demonstrated by this design for the ceiling of the King's Bedchamber Alcove (Fig. 144) at Greenwich, alas 'not taken'.

143 John Webb. Elevation of the cornice of the King's Bedchamber, Royal Palace, Greenwich, London, 1666. Pen (285 × 410)

144 John Webb. Plan of the ceiling of the Alcove in the King's Bedchamber, Royal Palace, Greenwich, London, 1666. Pen (290 × 435)

143

144

INTERIOR DECORATION

In any account of Colen Campbell there is one insoluble problem that concerns interior decoration: it has never been clear to what extent he was responsible for many of the interiors of the houses he designed. It is certainly odd that among the several hundred surviving Campbell drawings, all from one homogeneous collection, not a single design survives for an interior, apart from a few sectional designs such as for Mereworth and a few drawings made specifically for engraving. It may well be that Campbell contracted work out. What survives as evidence for an evolving style demonstrates that Campbell found it more difficult to achieve a Palladian manner for interiors than he did for exteriors. His section of Wanstead I published in 1715 (Fig. 145) is still in the late Williamite tradition of fielded and bolection moulded panelling with large inset paintings in the style perhaps of Ricci or Pellegrini. On the other hand, by 1722 he has adopted at Mereworth (Fig. 146) a Jonesian vocabulary, drawing upon the interiors at Wilton, the Queen's House, and, probably, Amesbury. His language is now more architectural, often bringing the elements of exterior architecture indoors, and it is this reflection of the exterior upon the interior that is most characteristic of neo-Palladian decoration in the 1720s.

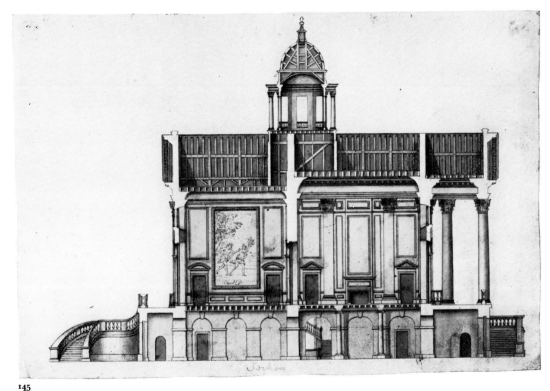

145 Colen Campbell. Detail from section through Wanstead House, Essex, as drawn for engraving in *Vitruvius Britannicus*, I (1715), plate 26.

146 Colen Campbell. Section through Mereworth Castle, Kent. Pen and wash (320 × 490)

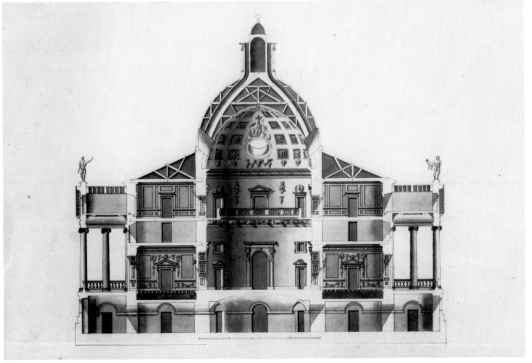

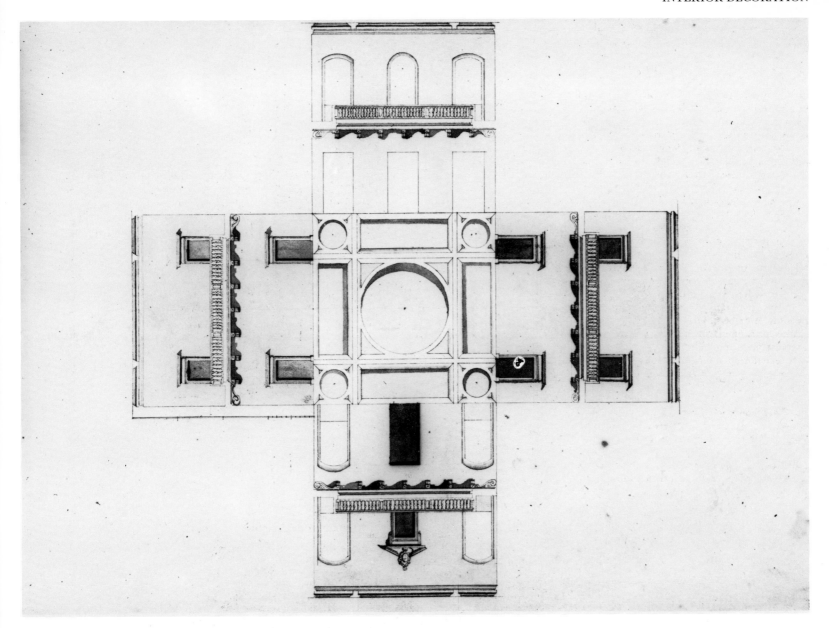

Campbell made this sectional wall design (Fig. 147) for the Stone Hall at Houghton, in about 1722 and must have intended it for engraving. This is innovatory in being the first single cube hall with its surrounding balustraded gallery to be copied from that in the Queen's House, and likewise the ceiling is derived from that source. Decoratively Campbell's vocabulary is not particularly Jonesian, but when he published the hall in *Vitruvius Britannicus* III, 1725, the programme had begun to change with the addition of a cove and sculptural

embellishment. A year later William Kent takes charge and converts Campbell's otherwise simply articulated scheme into a richly sculptured one, aided by the sculptor J. M. Rysbrack and the plasterer Giuseppe Artari. It may well be that Campbell's method was to provide the basic framework, to be filled in by the decorators, or in the case of a house like Mereworth, by the mural painters of wall and ceiling.

147 Colen Campbell. Plan of ceiling with laid-out wall elevations for the Stone Hall, Houghton Hall, Norfolk. Pen and wash (265 × 430). Prepared for engraving in *Vitruvius Britannicus*, III (1725), plate 34

148

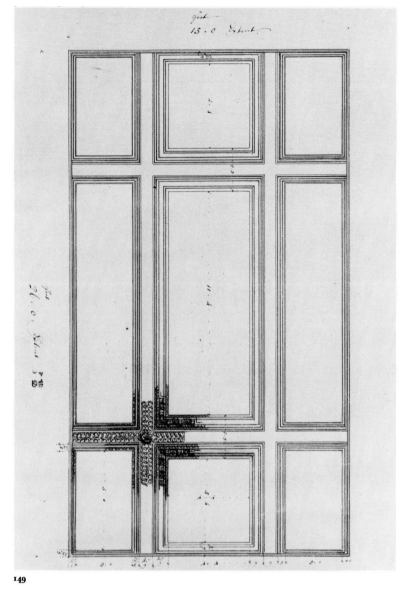

149

Despite the fact that Lord Burlington could have practised as a professional architect in his own right, and in so doing produced drawings and designs of a competence sufficient for execution by a builder or clerk of works, his method as a noble amateur was to use amanuenses such as Henry Flitcroft and Henry Savile. From the evidence of surviving drawings Burlington would prepare the first sketch, rather muddily washed-in, which would be redrawn following his instructions. The situation with William Kent is more difficult to rationalise, for Kent never made anything other than rough sketches, but as his authority was almost as great as Burlington's, there existing such a close intimacy between the two, it is possible that he ordered others to redraw his own designs. This plan and elevation (Fig. 148) showing profiles of the Blue Velvet Room ceiling at Chiswick is drawn by Flitcroft, but in execution was greatly enriched by Kent with painted decoration and ornamentation. This is one of the Chiswick ceilings whose source is not Jonesian.

The other design (Fig. 149), also drawn by Flitcroft, is for the Red Velvet Room ceiling, and here the sources are Jones himself, for Ware published this in *Designs of Inigo Jones and others*, about 1733, as an original by Jones, although it combines the plan of the Cabinet ceiling in the Queen's House with the beam ornamentation of the Hall ceiling there. Burlington reduced its size by half.

148 Lord Burlington *invenit*. Henry Flitcroft *delin*. Plan and elevation showing profiles of Blue Velvet Room ceiling, Chiswick House, London. Pen and wash (310 × 450)

149 Lord Burlington *invenit*. Henry Flitcroft *delin*. Section showing profile of Red Velvet Room ceiling. Pen and wash (305 × 410)

This transverse, north-south, section through Chiswick, belongs to a set of drawings prepared by Flitcroft and clearly intended for publication, although in the event only two plans, two elevations, and a section through the domed rotunda hall, were engraved for Kent in 1727. There is evidence that the completion of the interiors of the Villa was delayed, and that final details of the rooms in the main block were not finalised until the early 1730s. This particular section (Fig. 150) is through the suite of three rooms on the west side of the villa, from left to right on this section: the Blue Velvet Room, the Red Velvet Room and the West Closet in the Gallery. The chimney-piece overmantel in the Blue Velvet Room is based upon Jones's design for a chimney-piece at Oatlands Palace, whilst the Gallery closet chimney-piece is made up of an overmantel at Somerset House and a chimney surround for the Queen's House, whilst Somerset House designs are the source for the chimney-pieces in the Red Velvet Room. What is remarkable about Chiswick is the authority of every part of its fabric, irrespective whether that authority be original designs by Jones, his existing buildings, ancient and modern authorities such as Palladio, or Roman antiquity as conveyed by Desgodetz.

150 Lord Burlington *invenit*. Henry Flitcroft *delin*. North–south section through Chiswick House, London. Pen and wash (340 × 455)

123

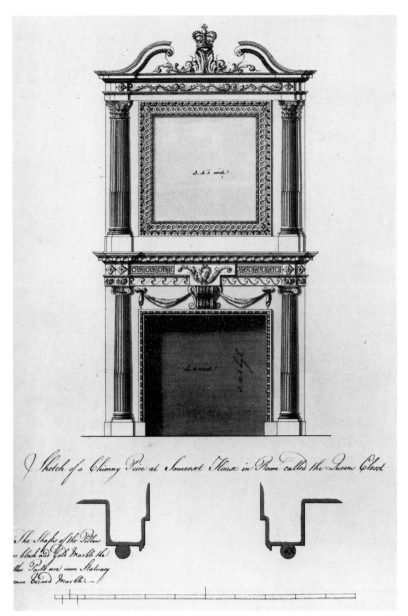

151

152

Apart from Lord Burlington's measured drawing of the Somerset House Chapel, no attempt seems to have been made to record the interiors of this palace before its demolition in 1776. Catherine of Braganza was the last Queen to inhabit it, and for most of its remaining years in the 18th century its apartments were used for a variety of purposes. It is not clear if these two drawings of chimney-pieces (Figs 151–2) are designs or measured drawings, but they are definitely 18th century, and are delineated in an Office of Works's hand. As both the Queen's

Closet and the Lord's Waiting Room were on the east side of the Lower Court, both may be related to work upon the royal apartments carried out in 1743, perhaps to designs by William Kent. Both chimney pieces are, in fact, high quality compositions, closer to Flitcroft's style, and are composed of a grammar of ornament drawn from authoritative sources. Here can be found the favoured wave mould, Greek key, and the guilloche.

151 William Kent *invenit*. Another *delin*. Plan and elevation of the chimney-piece in the Queen's Closet, Somerset House, London. Pen and wash (435 × 270)

152 William Kent *invenit*. Another *delin*. Plan and elevation of the chimney-piece in the Lord's Waiting Room, Somerset House, London. Pen and wash (435 × 270)

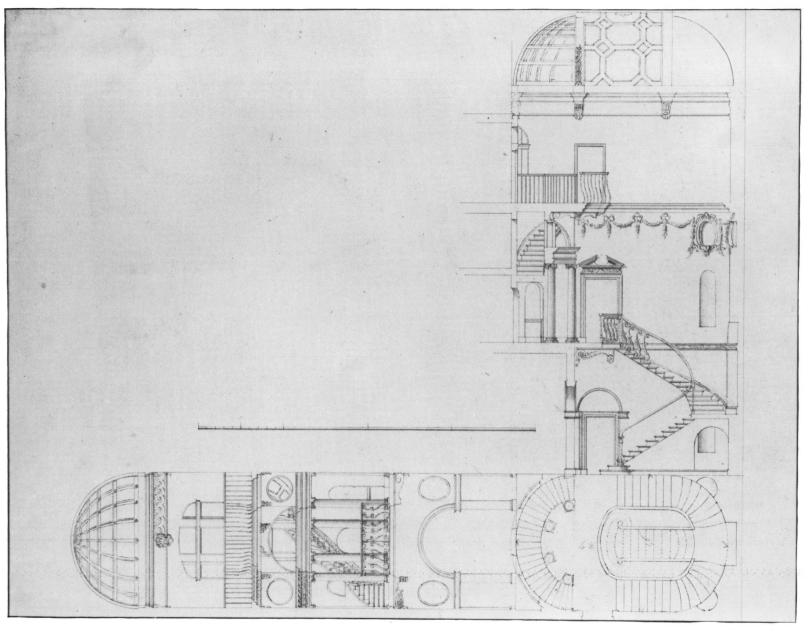

The neo-Palladian staircase was not generally of spatial ingenuity. The legacy from Webb was for flights of stairs climbing around a square or oblong staircase, or a spiral stair. It is therefore a surprise to discover in 44 Berkeley Square, built by Kent in 1742–46 for Lady Isabella Finch, a stair of such spatial complexity that there is really nothing like it in England (Fig. 153). It is as baroque as anything could be in its context and Horace Walpole hit upon the right description in calling it a 'beautiful

piece of scenery'. Its ornamentation is Palladian, but in planning and in the disposition of its spatial devices, it may owe something to continental models. However the screened apse echoes the apse in the hall at Holkham, itself an echo of the apse of Palladio's S Maria Maggiore in Venice, and there may also be a hint from the complex stair that Burlington put into Tottenham Park, Wiltshire. Kent's stair was hugely admired, and only perhaps equalled by Chamber's stairs in the Strand

Apartments at Somerset House, for which he would, if asked, have readily acknowledged his indebtedness to Kent.

153 William Kent *invenit*. Another *delin*. Plan and two sections through staircase in 44 Berkeley Square, London. Pen (470 × 362)

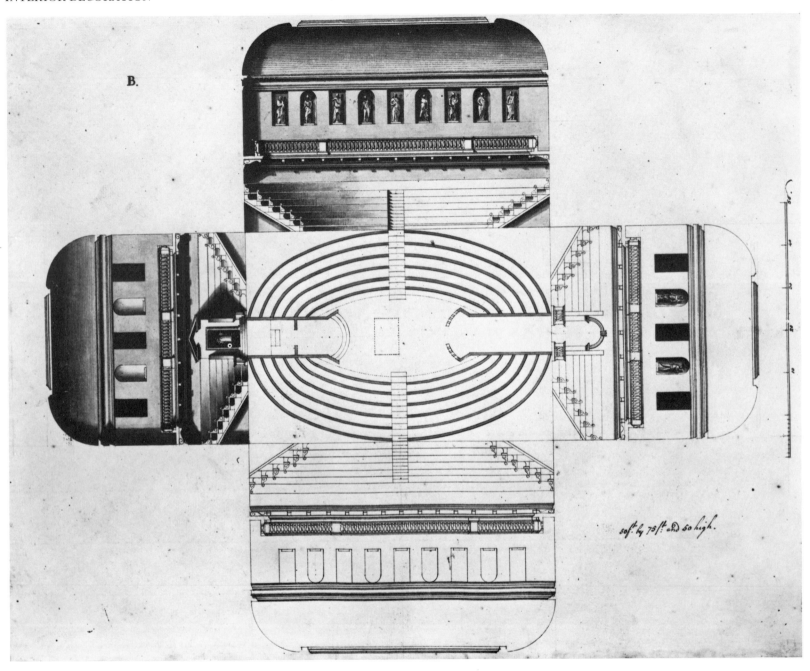

B.

soft by 75ft and 50 high.

This plan (Fig. 154) with laid-out wall elevations is marked B and is one of five versions for the House of Commons in the album of designs for a new Parliament House submitted in 1739. As the drawings are in a stereotyped Office of Works's hand, it is not possible to apportion responsibility between Kent and Burlington. The bleak austerity of the internal walls is in some contrast to the brio of Kent's remaining project for the House of Lords, so perhaps Burlington's restraining hand can be detected here. The Chamber is conceived as a gigantic anatomy theatre, combined with some hints from the galleried Banqueting House, in area 75 by 50 feet and 50 feet high.

154 Lord Burlington and William Kent *invenit*. Another *delin*. Plan with laid-out wall elevations for a project for the House of Commons in new Houses of Parliament. Pen and wash (350 × 445)

By the 1750s the Palladian domination was weakening, and interiors in particular were becoming rococo-tinctured, as illustrated by this section (Fig. 155) through a grand rotunda-type villa by John Sanderson. There is still a generic similarity to Mereworth or Chiswick, but the wall surfaces are now articulated in a more lively manner reflecting Sanderson's preferences for rococo ornament executed by plasterers. The spatial effects in this interior had it been built are, on the other hand, baroque. The circular rotunda hall opened up on the first floor with arcades and the barrel-vaulted saloon with a cross-vault between the two divisions, is frankly more in sympathy with the age of Hawksmoor than the years around the beginning of Sir William Chambers's and Robert Adam's practice. This is an example of the dilemma of second generation architects before the advent of neoclassicism.

155 John Sanderson. Section through a rotunda-type villa. Pen and watercolour (280 × 400)

As this design (Fig. 156) with laid-out wall elevations belongs to the Milton Abbey collection, it is presumably John Vardy's, for one of the interiors at Milton Abbey, Dorset, where he is known to have proposed designs in about 1755 for a new house. There is some evidence that Vardy may have decorated apartments in the old abbey house. Vardy was, of course, an officer in the Works under William Kent, and he it was who built the Horse Guards to Kent's designs after Kent's death in 1749.

Like Sanderson, he is a second generation Palladian who found himself compelled to compromise. He died in 1765, by which time he had been actively building Spencer House in London, witnessing there the installation of neoclassic painted interiors by Sames Stuart. As this design displays, the rococo was his milieu. He must have been well aware of the French-styled ornamental interiors at Norfolk House, St James's Square executed under Matthew Brettingham's supervision in the 1750s.

156 John Vardy. Laid-out wall elevation for a room proposed for Milton Abbey, Dorset. Pen (360 × 485)

Glossary of terms

Aedicule An opening framed by columns or pilasters and sometimes with a pediment, or often enclosing a niche (Figs 76, 138)

Apsidal Terminating in, or consisting of an apse, or semicircular wall (Figs 62, 102)

Architrave The base part of an entablature, or, more generally, the upper part of a frame for a door or window (Figs 138, 143)

Arcuated Consisting of arches, or using arches as the principal feature

Astylar Without columns or pilasters as in an astylar facade (Fig. 2; see also p. 37)

Barrel-vault A vault or ceiling of semicircular section, unbroken by cross vaults or ribs (Fig. 136)

Basilica In Palladian terms derived from a roman assembly hall, via Vitruvius or Palladio, and often having the form of an oblong rectangular building or room with aisles (Fig. 63; see also p. 38)

Bason In garden terminology, small geometrical pools of water

Blocked windows Because popularised by James Gibbs, called Gibbsian windows, often with heavy keystones and the sides broken by distinctive voussoirs (Figs 41, 103)

Casina A bath-house or temple in a park, often called a casino, and if containing a cold plunge bath, a bagnio (see also p. 19)

Concatenated Linked together; in Palladian terms explicitly a style favoured by William Kent in which units are linked together usually with advancing and receding of planes (Figs 61, 71)

Diocletian window Sometimes called a therm window, and derivative from a feature of the Roman Baths of Diocletian: semicircular windows divided by two upright mullions (Figs 57, 58)

Entablature The decorative feature surmounting a column or pilaster, and continued between them, and conisting in descending order of cornice, frieze and architrave (Fig. 143)

Facadism The method of treating the facade or elevation of a building

Guilloche A form of ornament or decoration consisting of bands interlaced to form a plait (Figs 51, 149)

Hexastyle Meaning a grouping of six columns in a portico, or tetrastyle with four columns etc (Figs 42, 57)

In antis Recessed into a building as a portico *in-antis* (see also p. 21)

Jacobethan Used to describe the architecture and designs of the late Elizabethan and early Jacobean periods in England, around 1600

Keystone The stone, often decorated, that forms the topmost element in an arch (Figs 11, 13)

loggia A building or feature in the form of a gallery open on one or more sides, often via a portico, row of pillars or series of arches (Figs 6, 62)

Nappa Italian for the chimney surround, rather than the overmantel above it

Patte d'oie Literally goose's foot, and in garden design descriptive of a number of avenues converging upon a semi-circle or open space

Piano-nobile The principal storey raised above ground level and demarcated as such on the exterior of the building (Figs 43, 46)

Palladian window Also known as a Venetian window (cf)

Rotunda A building, or internal space, usually four-square, and domed. In Palladian usage derived from Palladio's Villa Capra or Rotonda at Vicenza (Figs 57, 97)

Rule of taste Hogarthian in derivation, in the case of neo-Palladianism descriptive of that canon of architectural and artistic taste, or indeed of personal behaviour, pursued by the likes of Lords Shaftesbury and Burlington

Sala grande The grand reception or entrance hall; eg the Whitehall Banqueting House (Figs 145, 147)

Serlian Sometimes referring to the Palladian or Venetian window, and called a Serliana; but also to windows and entrances, notably those with voussoirs, found in Serlio's books

Venetian window Sometimes called a Palladian or Serlian window, it is tripartite in form, with the central opening wider than the sides and rising above them into an arch (Figs 39, 81)

Villa A small country house, usually the secondary seat of a landed family, often in a suburban setting but not necessarily so. The plan must be square, with a compact arrangement of rooms grouped round a staircase, and expressed on the two main exterior facades in a 1-3-1 rhythm of windows or bays (Figs 3, 40)

Voussoir The wedge-shaped stone or brick that is one of the elements in an arch (Figs 10, 12)

Bibliography of publications consulted

Beard, Geoffrey, *Georgian Craftsmen and their work*, 1966

Burke, Joseph, *English Art 1714–1800*, 1976

Campbell, Colen, *Vitruvius Britannicus*, I (1715), II (1717), III (1725)

Colvin, H. M, 'The South Front of Wilton House', *Archaeological Jnl*, CXI, 1954

Colvin, H. M, 'A Scottish Origin for English Palladianism', *Architectural History*, 17, 1974

Colvin H. M, (*ed.*) *The History of the King's Works, V 1660–1782*, 1976

Colvin, H. M, (*ed.*) *The History of the King's Works, III 1485–1660* (Part I), 1975 and *IV 1485–1660* (Part II) 1980

Colvin, H. M, *Biographical Dictionary of British Architects 1600–1840*, 1978

Colvin, H. M, & Craig, M, *Architectural Drawings In the Library of Elton Hall by Sir John Vanbrugh and Sir Edward Lovett Pearce*, 1964

Connor, T. P, 'The Making of Vitruvius Britannicus', *Architectural History*, 20, 1977

Connor, T. P, 'Colen Campbell as Architect to the Prince of Wales' *Architectural History*, 22, 1977

Connor, T. P, 'Architecture and Planting at Goodwood 1723–1750', *Sussex Arch. Collections*, CXXII, 1980

Country Life magazine: articles published weekly, *cf.* published cumulative index of houses etc.

Fowler, John and Cornforth, John, *English Decoration in the 18th Century*, 1974

Girouard, Mark, 'Ambrose Phillips of Gardendon', *Architectural History*, 8, 1965

Harris, Eileen, *Thomas Wright Arbours & Grottos . . . with a catalogue of Wright's works in architecture and garden design*, 1979

Harris, John, 'Inigo Jones and the Prince's Lodging at Newmarket', *Architectural History*, 2, 1959

Harris, John, *Catalogue of the R.I.B.A. Drawings Collection: Inigo Jones & John Webb*, 1972

Harris, John, *Catalogue of the R.I.B.A. Drawing Collection: Colen Campbell*, 1973

Harris, John, Orgel, Stephen, & Strong, Roy, *The King's Arcadia; Inigo Jones and the Stuart Court*, 1973

Harris, John, and Tait, A. A, *Catalogue of the Drawings by Inigo Jones, John Webb and Issac de Caus at Worcester College, Oxford*, 1979

Hussey, Christopher, *English Country Houses Early Georgian 1715–1760*, 1955

Jourdian, Margaret, *The Work of William Kent*, 1948

Kimball, Fiske, 'Burlington Architectus', *R.I.B.A. Jnl*, XXXIV, 15 October 1927

Kimball, Fiske, 'William Kent's Designs for the Houses of Parliament', *R.I.B.A. Jnl*, XXXIX, 6 August & 10 September, 1932

Lees—Milne, James, *Earls of Creation*, 1962

Lever, Jill (*ed.*) *R.I.B.A. Drawings Catalogue* alphabetical series 1968

Little, Brian, *The Life and Work of James Gibbs*, 1955

Mercer, Eric, *English Art 1553–1625*, 1962

Summerson, Sir John, 'The Classical Country House in 18th century England', *Jnl of the Royal Society of Arts*, July 1959

Summerson, Sir John, *Inigo Jones*, 1966

Summerson, Sir John, *Architecture in Britain 1530–1830*, 197

Stutchbury, H. E, *The Architecture of Colen Campbell*, Manchester, 1967

Survey of London (Greater London Council) XXXI–XXXII, 1963

Tait, A. A, 'Isaac de Caus and the South Front, Wilton House', *Burlington Magazine*, Feb. 1964

Whinney, Margaret and Millar, Sir Oliver, *English Art 1625–1714*, 1957

Wittkower, Rudolf, *Palladio and English Palladianism*, 1974

Index